"Jane Herlong is an extraordinary ⟨...⟩ substantive and whose style is infectious. In this book, she masterfully chronicles stories that touch your heart and tickle your funny bone!"

—Dr. Nido R. Qubein, president,
High Point University

"Jane has that rare gift of being able to write funny. I laughed from the first page right up to the last. I found the book totally delightful, and that's not a word I often use!"

—Larry Winget, *New York Times* bestselling author, social commentator, and television personality

"As a South Carolina girl who enjoys our beautiful beaches, I love the way Jane uses flip-flops to illustrate life's challenges and her sense of humor on how to sparkle through it all."

—Nancy O'Dell, co-host of *Entertainment Tonight*

"I love the way Jane Herlong highlights iconic biblical women and their flip-flops. This book is funny and insightful, and it offers sound advice for how, when life flips, to not become a flop!"

—Meredith Oliver, CSP, professional speaker, president & creative director of Meredith Communications, and author of *FANtastic Marketing*

"*Laugh-out-loud funny* and *heartwarming* are two of the many things I love about this book. We could all benefit from a little more wisdom, humility, and humor, and this is a book that delivers all three."

—Mark Sanborn, president of Sanborn and Associates, leadership speaker, and bestselling author

My friend nearly fell over at the abomination of it all, until I pointed out that the assailing shoes were blinged-out. How like another of my *belle friends* to note the importance of rhinestones on our footwear—no matter the style—especially as we women journey through this thing called 'life.' You'll laugh (hard!) at the hilarity of it all, but you'll also ponder the grace we, as women, have been blessed with."

—Eva Marie Everson, bestselling Southern fiction author, and author of *The One True Love of Alice-Ann*

"This book will make you laugh hysterically one minute and tear up the next. Packed with stories and anecdotes that anyone can relate to, *Rhinestones on My Flip-Flops* is a wonderful, inspirational journey that will make you love the path the Lord has laid out for your life."

—Eric Chester, award-winning speaker and bestselling author of *On Fire at Work: How Great Companies Ignite Passion in Their People Without Burning Them Out*

rhinestones
on my
flip-flops

*Choosing Extravagant Joy in the Midst
of Everyday Mess-Ups*

JANE JENKINS HERLONG

New York   Nashville

FaithWords
Hachette Book Group
1290 Avenue of the Americas, New York, NY 10104
faithwords.com
twitter.com/faithwords

First Edition: September 2017

FaithWords is a division of Hachette Book Group, Inc. The FaithWords name and logo are trademarks of Hachette Book Group, Inc.

The publisher is not responsible for websites (or their content) that are not owned by the publisher.

The Hachette Speakers Bureau provides a wide range of authors for speaking events. To find out more, go to www.hachettespeakersbureau.com or call (866) 376-6591.

All scripture quotations, unless otherwise indicated, are taken from the *Holy Bible, New International Version*®, NIV®. Copyright ©1973, 1978, 1984, 2011 by Biblica, Inc.™. Used by permission of Zondervan. All rights reserved worldwide. www.zondervan.com. "NIV" and "New International Version" are trademarks registered in the United States Patent and Trademark Office by Biblica, Inc.™.

Scriptures noted (ICB) are taken from *The Holy Bible, International Children's Bible*®. Copyright © 1986, 1988, 1999, 2015 by Tommy Nelson™, a division of Thomas Nelson. Thomas Nelson is a registered trademark of HarperCollins Christian Publishing, Inc.

Scriptures noted (NIRV) are taken from *The Holy Bible, New International Reader's Version*. Copyright © 1995, 1996, 1998, 2014 by Biblica, Inc®. Used by permission. All rights reserved worldwide.

Scriptures noted (NLV) are taken from *The Holy Bible, New Living Bible*. Copyright © Christian Literature International.

Scriptures noted (KJV) are taken from *The Holy Bible, King James Version*.

Library of Congress Cataloging-in-Publication Data has been applied for

ISBNs: 978-1-4789-7434-5 (trade paperback), 978-1-4789-7433-8 (ebook)

Printed in the United States of America

LSC-C

10 9 8 7 6 5 4 3 2 1

This book is dedicated to the greatest blessings in my life: my wonderful husband, Thomas, and my two children, Holmes Herlong and Caroline Herlong Turner. Thank you for giving me rhinestones of love and laughter as we continue to find joy in the midst of life's flip-flops on our amazing journey as a family.

contents

CONTENTS

rhinestones
on my
flip-flops

Chapter 1

I Did Not Want to Hear
This...Period!

Daddy had just tied the *Minx*, our little boat, at the dock on Abbapoola Creek. My heart was filled with a combination of summer memories and sadness as Momma and Daddy told us to wave good-bye to my favorite beach, Bird Key. Fall was in the air in the Lowcountry; change was coming.

Back at home, I sat on my bed fighting the tears; the summer fun at Bird Key beach was over. My thoughts were interrupted with, "Jea-un, I need to talk with you!" Momma's voice had a tone of urgency.

I sat at the yellow table and watched the hands on our clock. *When is my mother going to be finished with this "important talk"?* I wondered. My twelve-year-old mind heard only the words *once a month...body changing...*

Finally, Momma said, "Do you understand?"

"Yes," I lied.

"Okay, do you have any questions?"

"Yes. When does Daddy do this?"

The crease between Momma's eyebrows deepened— a sure sign I had stretched her patience to the limit. She said, "Daddy does not do this. He shaves."

But women shave too. "What do you call this thing?" I asked.

"It is your period," Momma replied.

Now that I have experienced this event and all the highly charged emotions that go with it, I think the name *period* needs to be changed to *exclamation point*. Girls should be told, "Once a month, you will experience your exclamation point," which sounds much more appropriate to me.

After that conversation with Momma, I told my BFF all the details I thought I knew.

"So how do you protect your clothes?" she asked when I finished.

Before I share my brilliant answer, let me remind you that back then only one feminine protection product was marketed: Kotex. "Momma says you wear a Q-tip."

My conversation with Momma introduced me to "the curse" and the word *cycle*. No more training wheels, skateboards, or pink bicycles with white banana seats. My childhood innocence was moving quickly into womanhood.

I did not like it one bit; it was my first major life flip-flop.

The reality is that our lives are one gigantic wheel of change. During adolescence, I was worried. I wondered if I would mature along with other girls my age and eventually look like the super-cute, older girls. It seems like once those changes start, our lives transition into light speed with marriage and children, followed by more interesting changes. And as life unfolds, we will experience inevitable challenges or flip-flops that can affect our sense of self, security, and faith.

Rhinestones on My Flip-Flops shows women how to thrive in the midst of life's changes and challenges. Prudent women search for living examples, or WOW (women of wisdom), as a how-to manual.

Iconic women of the Bible also give us instruction. Here is a partial list of remarkable ladies who have had some major flip-flops and rhinestone moments too: Deceived Eve; Domestic-Diva Martha; Fearless, Fabulous Esther; Mother-of-Nations Sarah; Salty Mrs. Lot; and Dynamic Duo Naomi and Ruth. Coupled with some modern-day ladies, these biblical women provide insights with their personal flip-flops.

I have learned from many WOW in my life. Do you surround yourself with great friends who teach you about handling stress, sickness, marriage, children, aging, and other things? I have my long list of girlfriends who give me sound advice whether I like it or not.

So strap on your sandals—Y-shaped, strap, or thong (for your feet, that is)—and let's walk the journey of womanhood. I can guarantee that you will get sand between your toes on this wonderful, terrifying, and exhilarating trip. We'll climb mountains, cruise into the plains, and plummet into some valleys as we search for our eternal heavenly summer. The unknown route of your journey can be rewarding and fulfilling if you pack your suitcase with humor and sound teaching. It's all about learning how to keep the sparkle and shine on our God-given talents as we experience life's inevitable flip-flops.

Chapter 2

Deceived Eve

Adam and Eve were the first people who failed to read Apple's Terms and Conditions.

Here is the account of the first family's major flip-flop:

When the woman saw that the fruit of the tree was good for food and pleasing to the eye, and also desirable for gaining wisdom, she took some and ate it. She also gave some to her husband, who was with her, and he ate it. Then the eyes of both of them were opened, and they realized they were naked; so they sewed fig leaves together and made coverings for themselves. (Genesis 3:6–7 NIV)

I remember my mother teaching Sunday school at St. Johns Episcopal Church on Johns Island. She was loads of fun and always had a unique perspective on Bible stories. Practically every Sunday, Momma would say in her unique Lowcountry brogue, "Chur in' repeat after me—Gawd is love" and "Jea-un, pay attention," since I was a convenient target.

Momma's lesson about Adam and Eve was "classic Eleanor." It went something like this: "Adam and Eve lived in the Garden of Eden," said Momma. "Gawd said, 'Adam, don't eat the fruit off this tree 'cause the day you eat the fruit is the day you gonna die.' Then Gawd told Eve the same thing. But the snake said to Eve, 'You want to be smart, then eat this fruit.' So Eve tasted it and so did Adam. Then they hid. Well, Gawd could not find them in the garden, so he asked, 'Where did y'all go?' Adam said, 'We are in the bushes.' Then Gawd asked, 'Who ate the fruit?' 'Eve did,' said Adam. 'Adam did,' blamed Eve. Then the snake said, 'Both did.'

"Well," my mother concluded, "Adam and Eve were so ashamed, they ran out the back door through the garden and jumped the fence. AMEN."

THE CORE ISSUE

My mother loved to color her stories with common sense and humor. She knew the basics. But when you look deeper into this story from the second and third chapters of Genesis, it is filled with the theme of this book: flip-flops and how we handle our mess-ups. The good news is that God is faithful to help us clean up our mix-ups.

We can learn a lot from the mother of us all, Deceived Eve. The serpent had Eve convinced that she would be like God and experience supernatural enlightenment. Oh, yeah, the crafty serpent left out the ugly details of her consequences. That shiny fruit had a nasty aftertaste.

Think of Eve as a dear girlfriend who is fixin' to make a bad mistake. You pray and seek wisdom to do or say the right words to help her avoid being deceived. Bottom line, you know this person is playing with fire. Do you know anyone like this? Or maybe you are dealing with a moral dilemma?

Remember the tale of the farmer and the snake from the *Fables of Aesop*?

A farmer takes pity on a frozen snake and brings it home. Thawed, the snake reverts to character and bites all. The wicked show no thanks.[1]

I bet that serpent in the garden had Eve so mixed up that she could have been convinced to count Adam's ribs just to make sure there was not another woman around.

My point is the enemy's greatest tool is deception, and many, beyond reason and common sense, fall prey.

I have been told repeatedly that in order to say yes to the laughter of a lifetime you first learn to say no to the passion of the moment.

No question, Eve was deceived. She even reclassified the forbidden tree by location instead of by what it is. She refers to the "tree of knowledge of good and evil" in Genesis 2:17, changing it to the "tree which is in the midst of the garden" (Genesis 3:3). Have you ever justified your thoughts by altering a few innocent details? Yep, I have.

IN A PERFECT WORLD...

When I think of Eve, I visualize her as drop-dead gorgeous—the ultimate Miss Universe, Miss America, Miss World. And she didn't even have to address the number one beauty queen issue: world peace. The Garden of Eden was the World, and there was eternal peace. The girl just had it all.

Eve also lived in an "all natural" world. Nothing was processed in the Garden of Eden. Just walk around in paradise and eat and drink whatever you want. If there had been a label to read, it would have said *Perfect*.

I started shopping at one of those expensive, natural-foods places. The free-range chicken breasts I bought cost $17.50. The supplier could have at least included a GPS route to find where the chicken roamed to justify the high cost.

> *"After God created the world, He made man and woman. Then, to keep the whole thing from collapsing, He invented humor."*
>
> Bill Kelly, "Mordillo"

In my mind, the Garden of Eden was like a holy nudist colony. Not only was Eve perfect, but so was her garden home. In "What Was Life Like in the Garden of Eden Before Sin?" Robert Driskell writes:

> *The world in which Adam and Eve lived would have been the perfect temperature, the perfect humidity, without pests or diseases, and without anything that would detract from their enjoyment of knowing God in a perfect, undiluted way. Surely, this is what is meant by the word "paradise."*[2]

DID ADAM WEAR THE "PLANTS" IN THE FAMILY?

When God questioned him, Adam blamed Eve. Then Eve blamed the serpent. What else could she do? There was plenty of blame to go around. So God said to both Adam and Eve, "Sorry, out you go."

The Scriptures also say Eve was attracted to a thing of beauty. God made her that way. Eve wanted to be wise, and she liked beautiful, shiny things. So that means it's okay to shop, right? But there was a deeper issue about to bite into Eve's character. The enemy used her natural attraction to beauty to entice her closer to disobedience:

> *When the woman saw that the tree produced fruit that was good for food, was attractive to the eye, and was desirable for making one wise, she took some of its fruit and ate it. She also gave some of it to her husband who was with her, and he ate it. (Genesis 3:6 NET)*

Sadly, Eve believed the lies of the enemy. Honestly, we fight the battle of the "shiny things" every day. Learn from Deceived Eve. This beautiful woman who lived in a perfect world made a bad mistake. Yep, Adam and Eve starred in the pilot episode of *Naked and Afraid*.

But even though Adam and Eve turned on God, He still loved them. We also see how God's heart was grieved and how passionate our Father is about fellowship with His children.

"The Lord made Adam, the Lord made Eve, he made 'em both a little bit naive."[3]

Yip Harburg

The New International Version states that Adam named his wife Eve because she would become the mother of all the living (Genesis 3:20). Is it fair to assume that Eve also knew more than the Lord wanted her to know? Have you ever contemplated that? I've matured enough to realize that sometimes not knowing is a healthy option. When someone wants to speak ill of another person, many times I do not want to know. Knowing that kind of information may pollute my mind. What if this person speaks ill of you? I learned a great lesson years ago: what others think about you is none of your business, so do not make it your business.

In *Bury Me with My Pearls*, I share some stories in the chapter titled "Dark Pearl" about a heart-wrenching time my family experienced. During all the drama, there was a family member whom I trusted. She was so loving toward my mother, and I felt very close to her. Several people warned me that she was betraying me. As my second momma, Tootsie, often said in her Gullah brogue, "Jea-un, bess not trust she."

I decided to focus on how well this family member treated my mother. Turns out, she was the kind of person who gathered information so she could use it against you. She admitted it was her way of being "in the know" and having "friends." Basically, gossiping made her feel wanted. Rather than recall how she deceived me, I choose to focus on her many acts of kindness toward my mother. This is an example of deciding to close your ears and mouth. Refuse to let unhealthy words and thoughts poison your mind, just like the forbidden fruit poisoned Deceived Eve's judgment.

THE FRUIT THAT BITES BACK

The biblical account of our first family is a tale of not-so-beautiful consequences. It is a story about making a split-second decision that can rule the rest of your life.

Beautiful Eve had a great husband and lived in paradise. But she wanted more. Sadly, believing the lie that she didn't have it all cost her all. This was "man- or womankind's" first major flip-flop.

What we as women learn about Deceived Eve is to beware of the lie that we need more of something. Be thankful for what you have and count your blessings every day. In the midst of temptations, serious mistakes can be made. You can recover with time, prayer, and the right people in your life. Let's face it, we all have flip-flops, but how we handle them depends on our level of commitment in developing godly character.

In Eve's case, she had to accept the fact that there was no going back. She had to adjust to a new life in a not-so-perfect land. Maybe she also had to learn how to forgive herself in order to adjust to her new life.

This story is about Adam and Deceived Eve's life-flops that flipped humanity, including deception, blame, consequences, and mercy. Always remember, in the eyes of our Father, there are no flip-flops too large to overcome.

In the midst of the mess-up, there was good news about our first family: "Unto Adam also and to his wife did the Lord God make coats of skins, and clothed them" (Genesis 3:21 KJV). How about that—God was merciful then and still is today.

There is no way I can conclude this chapter without mentioning my father-in-law's infamous toast he was asked to share at various weddings and other celebrations. "Daddy Big John" loved sharing this colorful toast that always made my precious mother-in-law, "Mama Jewell," blush:

> Here's to Eve, the mother of our race.
> She kept every leaf in its proper place.
> Here's to Adam, the father of us all.
> He knew just what to do when the leaves would fall.

Eve's Flip-Flop: She allowed herself to be deceived. She wanted more. Eve did not realize she had it all until she lost it all.

Eve's Sparkle and Shine: She gave us a gift, a "fruit" basket. Watch out for subtle deceivers, own your mistakes, and don't play the blame game. Bless Eve's deceived heart, she persevered and accepted her consequences.

How can you shine in the midst of your mess-ups? Remember, there are no flip-flops too large to overcome.

Chapter 3

Domestic-Diva Martha

*But Martha was distracted by all the
preparations that had to be made.*
(Luke 10:40 NIV)

MARTHA WAS A SHE: *SIDETRACKED HOME EXPERT*

Ever had someone super important invited to your home? It's the same story. "Well, I was cleaning out the garage and realized the trim needed to be painted...but that led to waxing the floor, which led to..." I have been so caught up in the details that I was too stressed to enjoy the visitor. Is it appropriate to say the devil is in the details? Both Mary and Martha were good women, but in all the hoopla, Martha was sidetracked and became a "stressed-out mess-up."

*As Jesus and his disciples were on their way, he
came to a village where a woman named Martha*

opened her home to him. She had a sister called Mary, who sat at the Lord's feet listening to what he said. But Martha was distracted by all the preparations that had to be made. She came to him and asked, "Lord, don't you care that my sister has left me to do the work by myself? Tell her to help me!"

"Martha, Martha," the Lord answered, "you are worried and upset about many things, but few things are needed—or indeed only one." (Luke 10:38–42a NIV)

Could this story be about the first female catfight? Bless her heart, Martha was a domestic soul. Not me.

- Dusting? Isn't dust a protective coating for furniture?
- Run the vacuum? I consider that heavy equipment, and I do not have a permit.
- Laundry? When I forgot to wash Thomas's socks, I sprayed them with deodorant, then threw them in the dryer on Fluff.
- Cooking? Have you ever thawed out steaks in the dishwasher on the Rinse-and-Hold setting? Guilty!

I love throwing in some humor, but the real issue with Domestic-Diva Martha is priorities.

Like Martha, I get my priorities mixed up. Mary just wanted to sit at the feet of Jesus and soak in His presence. Jesus' words in verse 42 are powerful: "Mary has chosen what is better, and it will not be taken away from her." In other words, Mary gets it. Unfortunately, we all have Martha Moments when we try to make everything perfect.

I am not a domestic diva—never have been and never will be. One of the best gifts you can give yourself is to learn quickly what you do best and stop trying to impress people.

I learned this lesson from hosting the Johnston Tour of Homes.

TOU-WAH OF HOMES

"Jay-yun, is this Ja-ne Herlong?" asked the stranger when I answered the phone.

"Yes," I replied hesitantly.

"Dar-lin', this is Eugenia Smith Edwards Holmes, and we are all here-a at our-ah monthly meetin' and would like to ask you to have your-a lovely home on tou-wah to raise money for . . . " Her accent was as thick as a pot of leftover grits.

"Your house . . . on tou-wah!" was all I heard. Everything would have to be perfect.

The magic of the moment was interrupted when my left-brained husband said, "We don't have any furniture."

Thomas and I were newlyweds and had spent the last two years renovating our old home. We had been given a historic house that had been empty for twenty years. We cut the house in two sections and dragged it across the farm. Ever since we made the investment to renovate, Thomas says, "The house owns us."

We had been married long enough for him to know that the glazed look on my face revealed a woman on an unhealthy, expensive mission. The community was coming to see our home, and it had to be fabulous.

My Martha mentality was in full swing. For the next several months, all I could think about was the tour.

"Thomas, fix this."

"Are the steps on the stairs okay?"

"Did you finish painting the bathroom?"

We had our disagreements, but I had my agenda. My heart beat one message: get the house ready.

With two rooms left to decorate, I decided to designate one of them the Christmas room. Why not put a big ol' Christmas tree in it and be done with it? I told Thomas to cut down a tree the size of the one used at Rockefeller Center in midtown Manhattan. He met the challenge and found a tree with three trunks. The tree literally filled the room. In fact, it was so big that it took three people and a chain saw to take it down after Christmas—in February.

A local decorator, Wayne, who knew everyone in the community, assured me the other room would look fabulous and told me not to worry about furniture. Two days before the tou-wah, Wayne arrived in a pickup truck filled with beautiful furniture and accessories and backed it up to my front door.

The house was perfect!

The long-awaited event arrived, as did the guests. I savored every moment until I heard one touree comment, "Why, isn't that Josie's settee?"

"Why, yes," said another woman. "And I believe that lamp and end table belong to Helen."

"No, that lamp belongs to Virginia because that was our wedding gift to her. But I am positive that chair belongs to Jewell."

I overheard similar conversations by the locals throughout the afternoon.

Busted. I should have known better. In a small town, everybody knows everybody's business and what belongs to whom. Wayne raided the homes of Edgefield's finest families. My home was an eclectic blend of everyone else's furnishings that had been relocated to my home.

After the hoopla died down, I was presented with a large red poinsettia—a thank-you gift for all our hard work. Thomas's left-brained head said, "It cost us a lot of money for you to have that flower."

For those few months, having the perfect home and trying to impress others became my focus. Although it was a special honor, I, like Martha, got carried away.

IN A PICKLE

I remember my mother saying, "I love to hear my jars sing!" Tootsie and Momma were teaching me a fine Southern tradition—the art of canning.

The entire house smelled like onions and vinegar. Cucumbers were cooked, seasoned, and boiled all the way to their final destination—sterilized Ball jars. In six months, these jars would be topped with pretty bows and proudly presented to special folks at Christmas.

As a young bride, I decided to do what other Edgefield County folks did—"put up" peaches. I followed the instructions carefully. I peeled, boiled, and added sugar and Sure-Jell. I placed the lids on the jars and loosely added the ring. I sat down and lovingly stared at my domestic creations. With great excitement, I waited for my jars to sing. I waited and waited and waited. Not a sound. There was not a single pop, tinging, nothing.

Practically every pantry I know is stocked with a delightful jar of something topped with a bow and decorative label that reads *Merry Christmas from*...Sigh. I felt like a failure. Christmas would be ruined...my pantry, empty. I was a disgrace to my Southern heritage.

Liberation came when I heard a speaker say to stop working on your weaknesses and focus on your strengths. Improving your strengths will help your weaknesses. Where has this person been all of my life?

Forbes magazine published an article titled "Don't Waste Time Fixing Your Weaknesses," by Ian Altman.

Altman quotes Lisa Cummings, CEO of Pinch Yourself Careers: "We have got to stop trying to teach fish to climb trees."[4]

I have an old, nasty, vintage box of Sure-Jell circa 1985 prominently positioned in the door of my pantry. Every time I swing that door back, my eyes fixate on that crusty package, since that box of Sure-Jell is a sure-fire reminder of "Jane, don't go there."

THE WREATH THAT KEEPS ON GIVING

Mama Jewell, my dear mother-in-law, was a domestic creature. In my opinion, she was the perfect blend of both Mary and Martha. She loved to study her Bible and take care of her family. She was an amazing cook and tried her best to help me learn domestic ways...*bless her heart.*

I was always looking for ways to impress Mama Jewell, so my first Christmas, I made a lame attempt to make her proud. I was going to do something domestic.

When Thomas and I were newlyweds, we had to be frugal, and I had to be very creative with our gift-giving. I decided to do something I knew nothing about—make fruit wreaths.

Let me digress and say I am not a crafty person. I never liked making crafts in elementary school. If ever a grade was given in Bible school for being crafty, I would have earned a big, fat F.

I was so proud of myself for stepping out of my comfort zone. I bought the wreath form, various pieces of hardware, and began my Christmas project. I stabbed apples, pears, and oranges, then added some holly for a special effect. I added pecans for embellishment. The finished product amazed me. Mama Jewell would be so proud of me for being creative and domestic-ish.

I drove to Mama Jewell and Daddy Big John's house to adorn their front door with my festive, fruity creation. My in-laws were very conservative and resourceful folks, I might add. I have seen my mother-in-law iron used wrapping paper and recycle a ham for numerous dishes until the bone finally made its way to the dog. When I presented my holiday gift to Mama Jewell, she did not react as joyfully as I had hoped. Hmm.

The next day I drove by my in-laws' home and was surprised to see that an apple was missing from the wreath. I assumed the resident squirrel had helped itself to the fruit. Like any good daughter-in-law, I replaced the stolen fruit.

Surprise turned into shock the following day when one-third of the wreath was missing. I would have to inform my in-laws that some wild yard creature was stealing the fruit off my beautiful creation.

At lunchtime, I sat down at the kitchen table and reported my finding to my in-laws. "There is some wild animal eating the fruit off the wreath I gave y'all for Christmas," I exclaimed.

"Well, honey," said my mother-in-law with a modest smile, "I just hate to see anything go to waste."

On the kitchen table I spotted a large bowl of diced fruit. There was no wild creature stealing the fruit; my in-laws were eating the wreath.

The memory of that experience many years ago makes me chuckle since I was trying my best to make an impression. Through the years, I realized that Daddy Big John and Mama Jewell were not interested in the fruit on the wreath. They were much more impressed with the qualities of the Fruit of the Spirit mentioned in Galatians 5:22–23 (ESV): *love, joy, peace, patience, kindness, goodness, faithfulness, gentleness, self-control*. They also loved and accepted me for being myself—the best gift of all.

PINK CADILLAC WRECK

Mess-ups and wrecks come to us in many ways. Martha became distracted as she tended to her list of domestic chores. She was frustrated and should have considered scrubbing away unimportant details. I bet she got on Mary's nerves too. She worked herself into a frenzy to make sure everything was perfect for Jesus. When this happens, we lose sight of what really matters. I have been in a similar situation and maybe you have too.

I knew in my heart it was the wrong decision. I was searching for a job or some way to make a financial contribution to our home. In a moment of weakness I did something I should never have done—sold makeup.

My Mary Kay date with destiny began as I waited in line at a local McDonald's. A complete stranger turned around, looked at me, gently held my face in her hand, and said, "I can fix you." I responded, "I didn't know I was broken."

She turned out to be one of a kazillion pink ladies who were passionate about everything from Mr. K facials to Mary Kay color palettes.

Now let me say that I have great respect for this wonderful company. I love the idea of operating a home-based business. But my Mary Kay cosmetic dilemma was that I was not passionate about the products or my desire to sell. All I could think about was driving a pink Cadillac and becoming a Mary Kay rock star.

Something strange happened to me at that first Mary Kay meeting when I won some bumblebee jewelry. Pinning that bug on my shoulder was like having Mrs. Walcox pin my Girl Scout crossover badge on my new green sash. It was my big, pink dream come true. Or so I thought.

Sadly, the makeup was nightmarish on my very sensitive skin. I was so disappointed after three different formulas were mixed specifically for me and my face still looked like a pepperoni pizza supreme. I had to wear another brand and pretend I was using Mary Kay. I learned how difficult it is to sell something you do not believe in and don't have the skills to do.

Even though the makeup did not agree with me, that bumblebee pin gave me enough motivation to book my first party. I told the hostess-to-be the Mary Kay rules: have the party in a cool room with some refreshments on hand, and so on.

I was all dressed up with my Mary Kay smile and all-important pink bag loaded with everything a face could desire: cleanser, exfoliator, moisturizer, concealer, base makeup, eye shadow, lip color, and lip gloss. I was ready.

When I arrived at the house, red flags popped up immediately. First, the house was located in a not-so-good section of town. And remember that "cool" room that the party was to be in? Well, it was hotter than Phoenix in August. My makeup melted right off my face. In the "cool" room were the following appliances: a refrigerator, hot water heater, freezer, dryer, and washing machine. Pick any appliance. It was in that room emitting heat. The majority of the guests were eighteen and under, with the exception of the grandmother. Remember the refreshments? They were covered with flies. All I could think of was my grandmother McElveen saying, "Every time a fly lands, it lays an egg."

To make matters worse, an old drunken grandfather sat in the next room, watching television. One time he yelled, "Hit don't matter how much o' that paint y'all put on yo face. Y'all is still gonna be ugly. You can't fix ugly."

To add to the tragedy in progress, a little boy ran up to me and grinned from ear to ear. He was cute until I studied his mouth. The child had no teeth, only pieces of skin hanging on his gums. I blurted out, "What happened to his teeth?" The grandmother said, "Well, he sucked the bottle too long. He ain't never gotten teeth." Finally, the grandfather and little boy left the house. One less thing to worry about. After all, the Mary Kay show must go on.

I proceeded to follow the rules flawlessly. I loaded the pink trays with all the latest Mary Kay colors and described each one in detail. We cleansed, we exfoliated, and we moisturized, and finally it was time for the highlight of the show—applying makeup.

"Okay, ladies," I said. "This is the eye makeup. Let's apply this to our eyelids." Suddenly, there was a chorus of oohs and aahs concerning the grandmother's lovely eye color. The grandmother got a little carried away and put lipstick on her eyelids.

Just then the screen door slammed, and the grandfather and little boy appeared. The toothless child ran up to me and grinned from ear to ear. Each nub was decorated with one of those chocolate candy footballs.

At the end of the show, I sold a tube of lip gloss and quit the business. What lessons I learned! Don't do something that is not in your genre of natural talents and gifts. I had a revelation, like stressed-out Martha, that jolted me to the truth. I also realized all the time I had wasted. True beauty is achieved when you exfoliate and cleanse your life with good teachings from the right source.

THE FLOUR OF PRAYER

This next story and prayer reminds me of Tootsie, my second momma, who baked delicious biscuits. As much as Tootsie tried to help me make her biscuits, she would literally fall on the floor laughing when my "rocks" came out of the oven.

Regardless of my age, Tootsie always made me a baby biscuit. That small gesture of love was dear to my heart and always made me feel special. That was the way Tootsie lived her life: she gave unconditional love and support to both young and old.

Although she could never achieve her goal of teaching me how to make her world-famous cuisine, her Gullah wisdom and unconditional love will live in my heart forever. Enjoy this wonderful analogy about making biscuits.

One Sunday morning at a small Southern church, the new pastor called on one of his deacons to lead in the opening prayer. The deacon stood up, bowed his head, and said, "Lord I hate buttermilk."

The pastor opened one eye and wondered where this was going. The deacon continued. "Lord, I hate lard." Now the pastor was totally perplexed. The deacon went on. "Lord, I ain't too crazy about plain flour. But after you mix 'em all together and bake 'em in a hot oven, I love biscuits."[5]

Lord, help us to realize when life gets hard, when things come up that we don't like, whenever we don't understand what You are doing, that we need to wait to see what You are making. After You get through the mixing and the baking, it'll probably be better than biscuits.

BLUEBLOOD OR BUST

I believe that if you don't learn a lesson the first time, you will keep getting that lesson until you do learn it.

We were visiting some friends who had moved into a quaint section of the Lowcountry of South Carolina. They were attending the Episcopal Church of the Village, and since I was reared an Episcopalian, I wanted to make a fabulous impression.

I wore my precious pink-and-green Lilly dress with matching flat shoes. I knew how to blend. Of course, my son Holmes had to dress the part too. He was too old for smocked clothing, so I found a darling outfit with suspenders, a striped shirt, and a precious tie. He looked adorable—and miserable. We were both dressed properly, and that was extremely important so we could impress the church ladies.

I delivered Holmes to his Sunday school class with

confidence that I had done my job as a Southern Low-country mother by trying to make an impression.

Yep, we made quite an impression.

At that time, Disney's movie *Pocahontas* had just been released. Holmes loved that movie and even dressed up like the characters at home.

After the service, one of the Sunday school teachers guided Holmes to the door of the Sunday school class-room. "Well," she said, "he has such an interesting name."

"Yes, his name is an old Southern family name that was passed down for many generations," I said, straightening my spine.

With a haughty inflection in her voice, the Junior League–dressed, blue-blooded Charlestonian Episcopalian said, "O-poo-kuh?"

More than likely, Holmes had insisted that was his name because of his fixation with *Pocahontas*. An added embarrassment was pinned on Holmes's shirt. Someone had taken a Polaroid of him with a lame facial expression and a silly grin. On the bottom of the picture, his name was written in uppercase letters: OPOOKUH.

I still have that picture, and it still makes me laugh. But it also reminds me of what is important.

Have you ever been there? Just like Martha, we work hard to make a great impression only to shoot ourselves in the foot.

SISTAH ACT

Another interesting verse in the Luke 10 passage is this: Martha said, "Lord, don't you care that my sister has left me to do the work by myself? Tell her to help me!" Can you imagine—even in the presence of Jesus, the only person who could wave His little finger and say, "I command you in my name to help your sister..."?

Jesus had His *say* but let the sistahs figure it out. This is especially important for women since we have to learn how to handle our emotions ourselves. Jesus wants us to develop godly skills to deal with whatever life throws our way. Emotions can deceive us, and they often become a weapon the enemy uses against us. Martha was frustrated with Mary. But woe to Martha; she was opening the door for anger, resentment, distrust, a critical spirit, and unkindness.

And then there is that horrible green-eyed monster called jealousy. Why is it called a monster? Because jealousy has no cure and knows no boundaries. Jealousy is a troublemaker for the person being targeted, but it is also a tormentor for the jealous person.

In many families, destructive emotions can erupt like a volcano and smother everyone with molten responses. It may be that one child has pent-up resentment over the years. Another sibling may end up being responsible for aging parents. This is a double-edged sword. Shame on the children who do nothing to help and pay no attention to their parents. To the child who does it all, I give this caution: watch your mouth. The enemy can destroy families when resentment builds. The focus should be the well-being of the parent, not unresolved, buried issues.

At times, I could have added a lot of stress to my aging mother's life, but I asked the Lord to help me watch my actions and words. It was hard. I failed many times, but I prayed for godly wisdom to know how to balance very difficult family issues.

In a way, Martha was fortunate to have Mary's behavior reveal what needed to change in her life. Wisdom is born when you listen and take action. Girlfriends, surround yourself with good people and those who care about you. Life is filled with unexpected issues and uncontrollable circumstances. How should we handle out-of-control emotions? If you are a fan of *The Andy Griffith Show*, Barney Fife says it best: "Nip it, nip it, nip it."

To me, the story of Mary and Martha is about balance and how to get back on track with prayer, good people in your life, and learning how to handle flip-flops. Their story also teaches us to isolate what we do best and reminds us of the price we pay when fitting in ain't fittin'!

GOD BLESS YOU, MY YANKEE FRIEND

I have a friend who moved from New York City to Edgefield, which she calls "Tiny Town." Linda is a genuine "New Yawker" who has lovely taste in clothing, always complemented with her pearls. Because she is a lady of style and taste, I decided to tote her to our version of high society.

Although I wanted to make a good impression on Linda, I was fearin' she would think I was totally tacky for inviting her to attend our small-town fashion show. For years, Linda was involved in Fashion Week at Bryant Park—the ultimate fashion event in New York City. Our version in Tiny Town is the spring fashion show at the Ponderosa Country Club. The emcee has a Southern accent that, if bottled, would be in great demand if any cared to take a listen. Some have said that this dear woman is more famous than Shealy's Barbecue. (If you are from our area, that is a big deal.) This wonderful, iconic woman can stretch mere vowels into four-syllable words.

In between wagon-wheeled tabletops and an assortment of other Western paraphernalia, the grand show began. As model Martha Louise Holsonback Rainsford Satcher from Virginia, Georgia, and South Carolina adjusted her outfit waiting for her introductions, the emcee said, "Hour-wah next model is originally from here-uh and has lived in the most celebrated Southern cities in the most exciting relationships... truly the kind of men and money we Southerners ador-uh... that we call unearned income. And we all know that she married well. A man who we all know is a card-carrying member of the Gifted Sperm Club. Well, Martha Louise

is back and making her-ah debut in hour-ah area...
again...since her-ah momma is in need of her-ah presence. So, let's welcome back hour-wah own Martha
Louise Holsonback Rainsford Satcher. Martha is grac-
ing hour-wah show with a new color this spring. It is
not green, ladies. Oh, no, ma'am. This color is kee-a-
wee-ah."

My puzzled New York friend looked at me and said,
"Is she trying to say *kiwi*?"

After trying our best not to snort in the most un-
Southern sort of way, Linda said, "I think I just pee-ah-
wee-ud in my panties."

Linda was a new friend from another part of the
country, who, unlike Domestic-Diva Martha, did not
try to impress anyone; she just fit right in enjoying our
entertaining Southern ways. Surround yourself with
folks who have a sparkly sense of humor; we all need
to laugh more.

SMOKIN' MOMMA

Nancy's mom was a smoker. Like a good daughter,
Nancy drove her mother to the local grocery store to
buy her weekly stash of food. And, of course, Nancy
knew that her mother would ask for the one item that
drove Nancy crazy—a carton of cigarettes.

The conversation was always the same. "Mother,
please don't ask me to buy cigarettes. I just know I

will run into someone from church. Really, I wish you would just quit smoking." As much as Nancy tried to change her mother, nothing worked. Just like Martha tried to change her sister's focus of being so heavenly minded that she, in Martha's opinion, was of little earthly good. Mary probably thought the exact opposite, hoping her sister would be more heavenly minded. Martha had the nerve to ask Jesus to say something to change her sister's focus.

Nancy's mother always said the same thing: "Nancy, you know smoking calms me down. Yes, it's a bad habit, but I enjoy smoking."

Honoring her mother, Nancy reluctantly did what she was asked. She stood in the checkout line hoping no one would see her buy the carton of cigarettes. Nancy also prayed she would somehow change her mother's focus on smoking and need for nicotine and instead adopt new coping skills.

Nancy's thoughts were interrupted with conversation from the excited checkout girl. "I just love your ministry! I am so honored to meet you. Can I have your autograph?" exclaimed the cashier.

With cigarettes in hand, Nancy turned around and stood eyeball to eyeball with television evangelist Richard Roberts, son of Oral Roberts. Nancy could not believe what came out of her mouth. "These are not my cigarettes. These are for my mother. I don't smoke. I used to smoke, but I quit since it is not good for you, and you know I was raised Southern

Baptist..." Nancy said she babbled on and on like a guilty sixth grader.

Richard Roberts looked sympathetically at Nancy and said, "Tell your mom that smoking will not send her to hell, but it will make her smell like she has been there."

The best part of this story is Nancy called me and laughed her way through the latest episode with her mother. We always loved comparing stories about our fun-loving and unique mothers.

The end of this smoker's tale is that Nancy's eighty-year-old Southern Baptist momma only lived a few more months. Nancy remembers that day with a smile. During those last difficult weeks, it's comforting to have had some holy levity and a sweet memory.

In the story of Mary and Martha, we know that Jesus' concluding comments were that Mary chose what is better. Did my friend Nancy choose well? I think so. Nancy was a loving and giving daughter who honored her mother. You know what? Nancy's momma is now enjoying a new fragrance in her heavenly home...maybe even in the smoking section.

Who are the Marys and Marthas in your life you think should change? Can you just love and pray for them where they are? This is a revelation that many times takes years to understand. So you decide—do you pray for them or pray for the wisdom to handle those you cannot control?

THE TITTIE BOOK

I was riding high. My third book, *Bury Me with My Pearls*, hit two lists on Amazon. It was both a best seller and a "hot new release." Wow! I got an F in writing in college. I wonder what Dr. Broome, my English professor, would think about this. Ha!

Can you tell from the setup that I was about as puffed up as a blowfish? Oh, yeah, I felt good about me.

I wheeled my car into the parking lot at our local IGA grocery store. I could not stop thinking about me. I walked into the store. Suddenly, from all the way across the grocery store, I heard a very loud, "Are you Jane Herlong?" Wheeling around with my head slightly delayed for effect (pageant trick), I responded, "Why, yes!"

"Oh, it is you," exclaimed the lady.

As expected, all heads turned to see me.

"Well, honey, I love your book," she yelled.

"Thank you so much," I responded with my head swelling in delight. I had written three books. My first book was *Bare Feet to High Heels*, and my second book was *What Ta-Tas Teach Us*. I knew, of course, she was referring to my latest, most fabulous work. "The Pearls book?" I asked.

"No," she said. "It's the one about them titties. Yep, I love that book 'cause it's funny and got lots of pictures."

Honestly, it sounded like I had written a porn book. My face dropped. Then it got even better.

"Yes sirree," the woman said. "You know where I got that book from?"

I was afraid to ask.

She proceeded to answer her own question. "I got it from a yard sale; it was a quarter."

If that is not funny enough, she ended the conversation by saying, "I did the math and figured I paid a little over twelve cents a titty."

It was a moment to reflect on trying to make an impression. This sweet lady gently and humorously reminded me not to get too carried away with myself.

If Martha were a Southern woman, she would have made sure all the townsfolk would have known about her famous visitor. And that she was working hard, much more than her dear sister, to make every detail perfect.

At the grocery store, after being so impressed with myself and thinking everyone else should be, too, I noticed I was appropriately standing by another reminder of my self-imploding thoughts—a canned ham.

Here is a word of warning—don't think too highly of yourself, and if you do, pray for folks who will remind you to not get caught up with yourself. We tend to ruin our service when we overestimate how important we are.

RED-FACED REDHEAD

Maybe this next story is more about humor than hair.

Thomas and I were invited to Dr. Lex Walters's retirement party, which was highlighting his thirty-nine-year tenure at Piedmont Technical College. It was a wonderful celebration honoring Dr. Walters and his service to our state.

I offered to sing a parody of Dr. Walters's life, adding some panache to the already wonderful evening. I also was asked to sing the National Anthem. So Thomas and I journeyed to Greenwood, South Carolina, for a special evening.

I always check to make sure I am ready to perform. The ladies' room was under construction, so I had to use the mirror of my small compact. I fluffed and sprayed my hair with a travel-sized red can of hair spray given to me by my hairdresser, Kerry. For some strange reason, my hair felt heavy and wet. I looked in the small compact mirror and panicked. The top of my hair was red—not sorta red, but bloodred. When that spray hit my processed hair, the spray turned into a reddish hue. My first thought was to call Kerry to schedule hairdo maintenance.

With cell phone in one hand and what I thought was Big Sexy Hair Spray in the other, I read the fine print on the can and realized that I was spraying Big Sexy Spray Tan on my hair instead of hair spray. Those cans look exactly alike.

I quickly grabbed paper towels and began rubbing the spray-on tan off my hair. My hands were red, my hair was red, and those paper towels were red. My hair was standing straight up like Phyllis Diller's hair of yesteryear. It seemed to become a deeper shade of red by the minute.

In the middle of the madness, Kerry called back. I had hung up my cell phone when I realized my beauty faux pas. Her words were calm and reassuring. She told me that the red would wash out and not to worry.

"Kerry," I exclaimed. "What do you mean, don't worry? I am singing for a couple hundred people in twenty minutes!"

Maybe my hair does not look that bad, I thought. Maybe this compact is so small that it exaggerates what I am seeing. Thomas will tell me the truth.

I searched through the masses until I spotted Thomas nibbling on a baby carrot. I got within twenty feet of him and his face said it all—not to mention that he laughed so hard he almost choked on the carrot.

And you know, things can get worse. I felt someone grab my arm and escort me to the front of the platform. I was seated with all the dignitaries, including many state representatives from across South Carolina.

Thomas was a big help. Every time I glanced at him during the program for visual support, he was in hysterics.

My only hope was to avoid sitting under the light and to remember my own words: the first person you must be able to laugh at is yourself.

I made it through the song, red hair and all. The good news is I sang the National Anthem, so I considered myself dressed for the occasion—I wore a navy blue suit with a white cami and topped it all off with red hair.

Kerry was correct. Big Sexy Spray Tan does wash out of your hair. I also washed away any presumption of feeling special. The evening was not about my singing, front row seats, or sticky red hair. I just had to laugh at myself while celebrating the accomplishments of a wonderful servant, Dr. Lex Walters.

Martha was focused on her home, meal, and making an impression. But the focus was celebrating the accomplishments of a wonderful servant, Jesus Christ.

THE WORLD WIDE WEB

"Oh! What a tangled web we weave when first we practice to deceive."

Sir Walter Scott

Mary and Martha were sisters. I am sure, like most sisters, their relationship was tested over and over again—from the Master entering their home and the sisterly spat that followed to the shortest verse in the Bible, "Jesus wept" (John 11:35), which refers to the death of

Mary and Martha's brother, Lazarus. I am sure both of these ladies were stressed to the max since Jesus was four days late after hearing Lazarus was graveyard/tomb sick (John 11:17).

All relationships have moments of being both challenging and rewarding. There are some relationships that remind me of this fabulous quote by an unknown source: "Friendship is like a violin; the music may stop now and then, but the strings will last forever."

And then there are the other kinds of friends; you know who they are.

One of the best analogies about relationships I have ever heard was from a sermon I listened to in high school. The minister told a story about his responsibility of pulling the curtain at a play during his college years. On opening night, he noticed an amazing work of art—a spiderweb. The problem was that the web was connected to the rope and the curtain. He knew that when he pulled the curtain open, the beautiful web would be destroyed.

The next night he noticed the web had been rebuilt; it was still beautiful but not quite as strong and intricate. As the nights of the production wore on, the spiderweb became more damaged and not nearly as strong as the previous one. The spider worked feverishly to rebuild and refurbish its beautiful web, but to no avail.

The same principle applies to relationships. If there is fracture, a breach of trust, the once strong and beautiful connection will be compromised. It may take years for the destruction to be repaired, and the relationship may never look the same again. Or your friendship could be permanently ruined.

When you choose to walk in a spirit that lacks forgiveness, you create a danger zone. Don't do this to yourself. Get over it and get over it fast.

My momma had some powerful quotable quotes. Here are two of my favorite quotes, which I call Eleanorisms: "Words never said are words never regretted" and "You can choose your choices, but you cannot choose your consequences."

Frankly, there are some relationships you need to get rid of. Some people you just outgrow. I believe God allows folks to come into your life for a reason, and when the goal is accomplished, it is over. In fact, God may be protecting you from a destructive future. Think of it like this: your EXIT from that relationship may reveal an opening for a brand-new ENTRANCE.

Get rid of relationships that burden you and people who are energy vampires. If you stop helping someone who can take care of himself or herself and you decide that enough is enough, the person you are helping will turn on you with a vengeance. Your "help" has actually crippled them; it prevents that person from standing on his or her own two feet. In a December 2016 broadcast, Joyce Meyer said something that stuck with me: "You can spend your entire life trying to help someone who does not want your help (just your resources) and ruin your life in the process."

Come on. Some people think they need a kazillion friends when it has been proved that only ten people will cry at your funeral. No kidding. Business consultant Scott Hansen writes the following:

> *When you die, on average, the amount of people that will cry at your funeral is 10, and the number one determining factor whether or not people will come to your burial is based on the weather. If it rains, only 1/3 of the people that were scheduled to go will actually show up.*[6]

So when it comes to healthy relationships, remember the fragile spiderweb.

Here is another suggestion that will help you choose the right folks in your life: you can either be the fly stuck in the web or choose to fly from the web.

DON'T STRESS WITH MOMMA

Thomas's cousin has four children—all at least two years apart. She walked into the kitchen one morning with one child in her arms and the three others clinging to her legs. In the middle of cooking breakfast, her husband stomped into the kitchen. He was not at all happy. "Look at my socks," he protested. "Once again, you folded a black sock with a blue one."

The overworked, underappreciated mother looked at

her hubby and said, "Well, black, blue, and brown all begin with the letter *b*. That's the best I can do. And furthermore, if you don't like it, you can wash your own clothes."

Weeks went by and our darlin' mother of four stuck to her guns. She even suspected that hubby had flipped his drawers inside out a few times since there was no evidence of laundry maintenance.

One evening, hubby came home with a sour look on his face. "Did you have a good day at work?" supermom asked.

"No," he growled. "I had a terrible day."

"What happened?" inquired our heroine.

"I was changing my clothes in the men's room on my way to work out at the gym, and my coworkers walked in and just stared at me."

"So what?" asked Wonder Woman. "They've never seen a man in his underwear?"

"Well," replied the husband, "I was wearing your panties."

No doubt, being a wife and mother has its challenges. But I take comfort and encouragement from the story of Mary and Martha.

This story is about two SHEs—one sistah was sidetracked and the other was more spiritually minded. We all need skills to help us handle our self-imposed flip-flops in relationships, communication, and priorities. Remember, these were good, godly sisters who simply had a difference in opinion. Martha was totally stressed and it flipped her priorities.

Our best weapons, or rhinestones, are to pray, do our best, and develop a holy sense of humor to deal with stressful events, things we cannot change, and our changing roles and responsibilities. My favorite "aha" lesson in this story is discovering the person God created you to be.

Now let's learn some lessons from the first ever beauty pageant girl, Esther. *There she is... Queen Esther...*

Martha's Flip-Flop: She tried too hard to make an impression. Her priorities flipped and her communication skills flopped.

Martha's Sparkle and Shine: She accepted her correction with grace and got over it fast.

How can you shine in the midst of your mess-ups? Keep your mind renewed with the teachings of Jesus and don't harbor bitterness. AND find your best self and be your "bes-test self."

Chapter 4

Fearless, Fabulous Esther

*Now the king was attracted to Esther
more than to any of the other women,
and she won his favor and approval
more than any of the other virgins. So
he set a royal crown on her head and
made her queen.*

(Esther 2:17 NIV)

I loved participating in the Miss America Pageant system. Someone told me once that I was like Queen Esther, who participated in the first beauty pageant on record. (It was so sweet to be called a queen.) Only later in life did I understand this powerful story that all women should read.

Esther is certainly not your typical Jewish princess. We can learn so many amazing life lessons from this woman destined for Jewish royalty. This story addresses God's perfect timing, Esther's wisdom, prayer—and egomaniacal men. Don't you know, Esther wore rhinestones or diamonds from the top of her head to the tips of her toes?

Submission and the role of women set the scene for this story since the reigning queen was dethroned and had to give up her crown. As we lament in the South—bless your heart, Vashti. This was an era when men ruled, and the entire culture depended on the inequality of the sexes.[7]

Personally, when it comes to being the head of the household—our kingdom—I do not want the stress. I have always said that I am not the breadwinner; I am the dessert winner. I also think of that wonderful movie *My Big Fat Greek Wedding*. Lainie Kazan, who played Maria Portokalos, said, "Let me tell you something, Toula. The man is the head, but the woman is the neck. And she can turn the head any way she wants."[8]

Don't you just love that? I think we can all agree that Esther was King Xerxes's neck.

Esther was also wise and listened to the counsel of her kinfolk Mordecai. When the king chose Esther, she was in his favor. But her cousin Mordecai dropped a bomb:

> *"Do not think that because you are in the king's house you alone of all the Jews will escape. For if you remain silent at this time, relief and deliverance for the Jews will arise from another place, but you and your father's family will perish. And who*

knows but that you have come to your royal position for such a time as this?" (Esther 4:13–14 NIV)

Esther was afraid but not in fear. Big difference. Fear can be paralyzing. She asked the Jewish people to fast, and God gave her the courage she needed to approach King Xerxes so the real bad guy could be exposed. Yes, Haman built the gallows for Mordecai to be hanged, but Haman "hanged" himself.

As the old saying goes, Give 'em enough rope…

Here's another interesting fact. Esther's Jewish name, Hadassah, means "myrtle." A myrtle tree's leaves only release their fragrance when crushed. Her heroism only appeared when she and her people were in danger.[9]

Okay, women, this is powerful: our fragrance is released when crushed. So when that happens to you, please don't be stinky! Be a heroine with a pleasant scent and use your sense.

AND THE WINNER IS…

Let the king appoint commissioners in every province of his realm to bring all these beautiful young women into the harem at the citadel of Susa. Let them be placed under the care of Hegai, the king's eunuch, who is in charge of the women; and let beauty treatments be given to them. (Esther 2:3 NIV)

Woohoo! I just knew pageants were in the Bible. Cosmetics, beauty treatments, and even a pageant consultant named Hegai. I connected with fun-loving guys and experienced women who helped me and many others shine and keep the all-important sparkle. No kidding. It is a pageant term: competitors must keep their sparkle.

No matter what new challenge you encounter or what new venture you enter, seek out the experts. I did. His name was Billy Harris.

WALKING WITH THE DEAD

In our state, only one man could help queens achieve perfect poise. Pageant gurus claim his technique was the best in the South, and perfecting it took years of practice and discipline. Folks said he had so many winners he lost count. His accolades included the likes of Little Miss Saturday Afternoon at the Mall to Miss Universe. If Billy had been living during Esther's time, he would have been in the king's court, coaching the wannabe queens on their quest.

One would think Billy's place of business would be located in one of those bridal/pageant shops that dot our Southern landscape. No, to receive a PhD in poise, the queens lined up in procession to Billy's funeral home.

To say Billy was the master of the human body is

an understatement. Dead or alive, he was good at his trade. Billy used his funeral home tricks to remedy pageant girl atrocities. He boasted about the big plug of wax he used to fill a hole in Ann Marie Smith's leg—an injury she sustained in a childhood accident. And for a finishing touch, Billy pressed a paper towel over the area to give the wax a porous look. He pioneered the fine and delicate art of wearing medical tape instead of underwear or "drawers," as they are more commonly known in the South.

Twice a week, I faithfully traveled 180 miles to Sumter, South Carolina, dressed only in a leotard, high heels, and a smile. All day I did one thing: walk.

"Ankles together, drop back, half turn to the right, half turn to the left, full turn, quarter turn, right stance, left stance, hesitation, line up," Billy commanded as we negotiated our living bodies between caskets, urns, and "Jesus Called" telephone-shaped wreaths. Billy had set up two huge mirrors: one in the casket room and the other in the "grievin' family room."

With all the hours I spent walking, I'm sure I could have traveled to Atlantic City and back. Billy had two rules at the funeral home: (1) When the doorbell rings, run and hide, and (2) always call before you come in case there's a dead body.

I never ate before I went to see Billy because the first thing he did was get out his trusty tape measure. He kept strict records about each girl's size. For lunch, I gnawed on hamster food while he ate a Big Jim Double

Chili Cheeseburger and a large order of cheese fries. He probably ate that stuff just to test my willpower.

It was particularly tough when Monta walked with me. Monta—her name alone conjures an image of someone with perfect beauty. She was gorgeous and had a fabulous figure. Nothing was "sto' bought." I was Miss Charleston and she was Miss Hickory. We talked about being in the Miss America Pageant together. Billy was so proud when we both won our state titles.

Yes, Billy was the master. He taught me volumes about how good bodies can look—dead or alive. God love him, Billy Harris helped me find my shine, which led me to the runway of the Miss America Pageant. I guess you can say that Billy was my equivalent to Esther's Hegai.

HEY, SWEET THANG!

We all need an encourager, and I am sure Esther had plenty of folks, like her adopted daddy, Mordecai, who challenged her on her journey. My encourager was a very colorful character named Big Red. Every time I hear the words *sweet thing*, I think of my pal Red.

One hot July day in the little town of Gaffney at the South Carolina Peach Festival, I met Big Red. It's right easy to catch a visual on this one...Big Red. First of all, you know he is big, and second, his hair is a deep shade of Tang. With a name like his, you can bet he is packaged extra friendly.

I heard Red, not to be confused with *heard of*, before I ever saw him. A blast from an "ooohga horn" heralded his entrance onto Main Street in Gaffney. Around the corner, Red maneuvered his white late-model Cadillac with bloodred leather interior. Before I knew it, he was swinging queens around, calling us all "sweet thang" and handing out packs of Big Red chewing gum and silver dollars.

Everyone was pretty much running for cover except me. He may have acted like a bulldog, but to me Red was all puppy. We wrote each other several times, and he sent me pictures of himself posing with Playboy bunnies at various NASCAR events. We were both looking forward to seeing each other at the Miss Southern 500 Pageant.

Labor Day weekend arrived, and all of us queens met in Darlington, South Carolina, for the festival. The director of the pageant warned us about a pesky character who loved beauty queens. I thought, well, that takes care of the entire male population.

The director said, "His name is Red. Do not speak to him. Speaking to him may keep you from winning the title of Miss Southern 500." What? Not sweet, innocent Red. No way was I going to avoid him.

Minutes later, I heard Red wheeling his white Cadillac through the parade route trying to find me. I hopped down off my float and gave him a big ol' hug.

Fast-forward with me, one year later. It is Saturday morning. We are in TV rehearsals at the Greenville Memorial Auditorium. That night, a new Miss South Carolina would be crowned. We were all clueless about who was in the lead except for the preliminary winners.

My thoughts were interrupted with a shout of, "Miss Charleston, telephone!" I thought that was weird since pageant contestants are never allowed to receive calls. Answering the phone, I heard the familiar, "Hey there, sweet thang!" It was Red.

"Well, darlin', I just talked to your chief judge. You see, me and him go way back. I told him you was a real sweet thang, and you had always been nice to me. I told him that he should pick you tonight to win. He told me you was gonna win, and so I just wanted to be the first to congratulate our new Miss South Carolina. Bye, now."

I dropped the phone.

Red was the last person I thought would know one of the judges. Did it really make a difference in my winning the pageant? Probably not. It made me feel good, though, knowing I treated him like my parents taught me. Actually, Red taught me a lesson. You never know who will cross your path in life, so treat folks the same way you want to be treated regardless of who they are. I also know that you pass the same people going up as you do coming down.

PULLED TO REALITY

Do you ever feel like you are living out the lyrics of Mary Chapin Carpenter's song "The Bug"? Sometimes you're the windshield; sometimes you're the bug. This is life in a nutshell. There will be those days when you have your act together and then the days when "that dawg don't hunt." I think it keeps us in balance. I had a similar experience that I call a dose of glamour and a slice of humble pie.

Many years ago, when I was Miss South Carolina, I participated in three parades in one day. Totally fatigued, I decided to break my rule of looking queenly. I put on a pair of jeans and removed my makeup—a true Plain Jane look. It was one of those days when I had traveled far beyond feeling like "sometimes you're the bug." It was more like "sometimes you're the statue; sometimes you're the pigeon." I felt like the statue.

Speeding down I-26 on my way to Charleston, I heard the sound of a siren approaching behind me... again. Yes, it was what I feared. "Driver's license and registration, please, ma'am," said the highway patrolman in a deep voice. All I could think of was how much trouble I would get into with the Miss SC pageant folks. I was driving a car given to me to use during my reign, so this was not a good thing. On top of that, I looked like the Hag Queen.

I gingerly handed the officer my license and registration. He walked back to his car, which is never a good sign. He came back to my car and handed me a warning. I was so delighted that I handed him my official Miss South Carolina picture in full beauty queen mode—crown, gown, and makeup. "Thank you so much! This is for you!"

He took the picture and stood for a moment staring at the queenly photo. He removed his glasses and looked even closer. Then he looked at me and said, "Doggone. Do you know her?"

FROM FLIP-FLOPS TO HIGH HEELS

Once upon a beauty pageant, or twenty pounds ago and eight skin cancers ago, I walked across many stages in high heels all the way to the Miss America Pageant. Swimsuit was my worst phase of the competition, so I had to shape up, literally.

Through the years, when pageant season is in full swing, we shoulda-been-queens love to post lots of photos from yesteryear on Facebook. I have not forgotten how tough it was to get in shape for my competition swimsuit figure. Having to walk half naked in front of a whole lot of people will make you shape up!

I have always said that pageants are life on steroids, since the Miss America program focus is on self-improvement. Esther had to make herself attractive to King Xerxes, so let's take note to be attractive to our heavenly King. The book of Esther reminds me of the following lessons I learned about being successful in life as I prepared for my most challenging phase of competition. I quickly realized that how I presented myself in the dreaded swimsuit competition (now called Lifestyle and Fitness) was a reflection on how I felt about myself.

1. Take advice from people who have your best interest at heart.

I stepped out of the dressing room wearing my first competition swimsuit. My mother and the shop owner stared at my thighs. "Oh my," exclaimed the shop owner. My mother translated, "Colonel Sanders would make millions from your thighs." They told me the truth.

Do you listen and learn from the folks who really want to see you improve?

2. Your weaknesses will catch up.

I could sing, I had good stage presence in my gown, and my interview was good. But there was a problem. My swimsuit score would hold me back from making the final ballot. I became serious about working out.

Isolate what is holding you back from achieving your personal best.

3. Passion drives people to do what it takes.

I was passionate about getting in shape. I ran down our dirt road dodging farm tractors, worked out at the gym, and paid for a treatment to get rid of fat thighs. I heard of a shop in Beaufort, South Carolina, that offered a strange procedure to reduce the size of thighs. So once a week I drove to Beaufort and had my legs wrapped in gauze and sprayed with this pink stuff.

Passion for becoming your personal best will drive you to discover your personal best. Don't give up.

4. *Check out what the competition is doing.*

There was a famous store that specialized in swimsuits. The shop owner assessed your figure and fit you to the perfect swimsuit. The challenge was that the shop was in Chicago. No problem. I flew to Detroit to visit my beau and had a long layover in the Windy City.

These unconventional efforts give you confidence to succeed. I promise, it works!

CONFIDENCE CREATES MAGIC MOMENTS

I did not win swimsuit, but my goal was to score enough points to get on the ballot. That is exactly what happened. Not only that, but I also heard my name announced later that evening: "And the new Miss South Carolina is...Miss Charleston, Jane Louise Jenkins!" It was magical.

I think Esther embraced these life lessons to hear her name announced as the queen. But never forget to shape up your sense of humor along the journey.

You may ask, "What about now, Jane? How do you handle not having a swimsuit figure after all these years?" I have developed a new way to have confidence when I wear my swimsuit: I find the most overweight person wearing a swimsuit and sit by her—or him.

Always be able to find the humor in life. It is good for your heart and soul.

FLOATING FRIENDS

Competing onstage in a swimsuit is very challenging to say the least! Esther may have been naturally beautiful, but I had to buy some support. I am not exactly 36-23-36. But there are lovely little helpers that can give you the hourglass figure needed to compete.

You can fake it at Miss America but not in the Miss USA/Miss Universe system. They actually have designated personnel that check your swimsuit and evening gown to make sure it is all you. Most men would pay to have that job.

However, there should be a warning attached to wearing such enhancers: "Do not jump into a swimming pool or jump off a diving board while using. This can cause embarrassment." This is firsthand info. Believe me.

When Thomas and I went on our honeymoon, I decided to pack my Miss America swimsuit and, of course, my accessories. After all, I was attached to them.

After getting the attention of all eighty-five honeymoon couples basking around the pool, I jumped into the water. The look of horror on Thomas's face as I surfaced said it all. Panicked, he gestured for me to turn around. Yes, there they were like two jellyfish (or, should I say, foam fish), bobbing on the wake. My little cone-shaped friends were right behind me. They made it to the surface before me. You would think that moment of embarrassment would serve to teach a lesson on what not to do, but nooooooooo—only minutes later it happened again.

Thomas overheard a guy, who was also on his honeymoon, say, "Man, I feel sorry for him," referring to Thomas.

Right after that I returned to Atlantic City for the Miss America Pageant and told the story to my good friend Donnie Smith. He laughed so hard I thought I was going to have to drag him off Atlantic City Boulevard. I said, "Promise you won't tell anybody that story!"

He said, "Oh, Jane, you know me. I can keep a secret!" Within hours, people from every state in the union burst out laughing when I walked by.

AGING UN-GRACEFULLY

Before a young woman's turn came to go in to King Xerxes, she had to complete twelve months

of beauty treatments prescribed for the women,
six months with oil of myrrh and six with per-
fumes and cosmetics. (Esther 2:12 NIV)

Esther and I are kindred spirits. I prepared twelve months before competing for the title of Miss South Carolina, and like Esther I was chosen.

When I was the newly crowned Miss South Carolina, the local television station contacted my family for an interview. Thankfully, Daddy left the house before the television crew arrived. The last time an "important stranger" had come to the house was when Momma hired a decorator who insisted that Daddy's pride and joy, his mounted mako shark and sailfish, "had to go." My shy, introverted father replied, "The only thing that has to go is you." That was in 1962. The fish are still hanging on the wall.

With Daddy occupied elsewhere, I knew things would go smoothly with the interview. When the television folks arrived, Momma and I were on our best behavior. Sitting in the living room, the attractive TV chick asked my mother, "How will Jane age?"

My mother said, "Jane will age gracefully."

I thought, *Really?* I will be dragged kicking and screaming *ungracefully*.

I was correct.

The truth is, I hate fat, cellulite, wrinkles, sagging skin, and those weird age spots that pop up whenever and wherever. Come on, who likes to look old? You should see my vanity area. Maybe I should say you can't see my vanity area since it is covered with anti-aging everything.

Let me cut to the bottom line. Within reason, if you invest in looking better and feeling better, good for you! We all need a good dose of self-esteem, and it supposedly comes from husbands. I have a wonderful husband, but I have to tell him what to say. No kidding. I say stuff like, "Don't I look good? Now you say that back to me, Thomas." I don't care; I take it however I can get it.

Well, Jane, you may be thinking, *that is simply vanity.* Maybe, but I think it is healthy mentally if you don't go overboard. There is Scripture suggesting that we take care of ourselves, ladies. For example, 1 Corinthians 6:19 says, "Do you not know that your bodies are temples of the Holy Spirit?" So keep your bricks, mortar, and walls from falling down. Remember Proverbs 31:22? "She maketh herself coverings of tapestry; her clothing is silk and purple" (KJV). She wore purple—a color reserved for the wealthy and for royalty in biblical times. We are all royalty since we are children of God.

Remember Deceived Eve? The Bible tells us that she was attracted to a thing of beauty. Well, so am I. Genesis 3:6 says, "She saw that the tree was beautiful" (ICB). Is it okay to assume that maybe...we just can't help it? I love trying to stay fit and fabulous like Queen Esther. This is one way we keep shining, ladies.

BIG HAIR IN TEXAS

My friend Lee Ann is quite a gal. She is beautiful inside and out, funny, and down-to-earth. She makes no apologies that she is constantly looking for ways to be fit and stylish.

This is the attitude of a modern-day Esther. To win the king's approval, Esther had to look and act like a queen. This is the "act as if" principle. Don't you know that Esther was a bundle of nerves? But in order to approach the king, she had to develop a confident, bold, and beautiful spirit. I bet Esther made a decision to act the part on the outside and prayed that it caught up with her on the inside. I have been there.

A few years ago, my wonderful hairdresser John had a bout of depression. All of us who counted on him to color and maintain our hair were fighting our own version of depression since we were all looking rough. Our code phrase for color was "the skunk is showing."

We all love John, but we could not wait any longer for him to show up. I made my appointment with another hairdresser. Unfortunately, a chemical was added to my hair and it puffed up like Don King's. *No problem*, I thought. *I can wash out this big hair*. But when I did, it puffed right back up. Unfortunately, my hair faux pas coincided with my birthday and driver's license renewal picture.

I ran into Lee Ann. She took one look at my hair

and said in her Southern drawl, "Honey, what has happened to your hai-ah?"

I told her the story, detailing the horror of needing to have my picture taken for my driver's license. I will never forget her response.

"Oh, Jane! You cannot have a new photo made. Yo' hai-ah is so big it will not fit in that little picture! Her-ah, look at my driver's license picture. It is fabulous!" Lee Ann had taken her old picture and glued it on top of her new photo. "It is a shame the motor vehicle people don't send proofs," she lamented. "Jane, honey, I am telling you the truth. I know you, and for fo-ah year-ahs when you hand yo-ah driver's license to strangers, you will tell the whole sad story…"

Lee Ann was right. I decided to wait until John got out of his funk and fixed my hair for the all-important picture.

The problem was, I had a speaking engagement in Texas. Not thinking my expired license would be an issue, I was going to fly out before my birthday and fly back the day after. Handing my license to the agent at the counter, he took one look at the date and said, "Lady, you are not going anywhere. Your driver's license is expired. In fact, you will have to get someone to fly here and drive you home."

I was stunned. I kept telling myself, *Don't panic. Think.* I said a silent prayer, and my "answer" showed up only minutes later—a gate agent change. A tall, 100 percent Texas Diva in full makeup made her appearance.

I knew what to do. It took courage but I got in her line, handed her my driver's license, and talked about her jewelry. I even sang a verse or two of a Texas favorite, "The Yellow Rose of Texas." I was operating on the "act as if" principle and did everything I could think of to divert her attention from the date on my license. Across the counter came the most beautiful white slip of paper ever—my boarding pass.

As I turned to walk away, I heard, "Ma'am." Oh no, I was busted. With my heart pounding, I turned around, expecting the worst.

The Diva gave me a big Texas grin and said, "I love your hair-ah!"

A QUEEN IN THE ER

"Just when you think the worst is over...," I told my audience at Ashley River Baptist Church in Charleston, South Carolina, concerning my previous twenty-four hours of stress. I tried to make the events sound funny, emphasizing how well I had handled everything. How was I to know the events to come in "pageant world" would make the earlier twenty-four hours seem like nothing? Proving once again that life is all about your attitude and a shining sense of humor.

After I spoke at the church, I was on my way to celebrate the conclusion of pageant week. All of us queens from yesteryear gussied up for a blast from the past—

even for a few seconds of walking and waving on the stage. Reminds me of a plaque someone gave me that makes me laugh: *We can't all be the queen. Some of you have to sit on the curb and wave as I go by.*

Pageant world is fun. I had been asked to conduct preshow television interviews with some prestigious women in South Carolina's government and to discuss the changing pageant-world styles as well as share the pageant's involvement with Children's Miracle Network.

I was dressed by one of the "greats" in pageant world for my TV appearance that evening, complete with blown-out hair, false eyelashes, and way too much padding in the top of my dress. I sparkled like the fake rhinestones on my beautiful Gregory Ellenburg gown.

The only problems were my predictable aching feet and the unpredictable, strange sensation of pain in the base of my hand. The pain increased as the evening wore on.

I knew I was in trouble when the newly crowned Miss South Carolina took her first walk, and the pain in my hand was so bad that I couldn't even clap.

My mind raced. I had a ten o'clock flight to Indianapolis the next morning for a speaking engagement, so my situation was not good. With throbbing hand and tired feet, I asked the security guard at the auditorium the question I did not want to ask. I had no choice. Dressed in my pageant-world overly padded gown, fake eyelashes, and blown-out hair, I asked, "Where is the nearest ER?"

His answer was real and honest. "There's an ER only

blocks from here. But I don't think you should go there since you'll look like all the 'escort' women at this hour of the night." In other words, outside the auditorium, pageant world ended and call-girl world began.

I decided to drive back to the Edgefield County ER to receive treatment from the locals who knew me and what my real job was. With rhinestone dangly earrings, I sat in the small ER waiting room. The door opened and a young physician walked into the room looking at my admittance papers on his clipboard. When his eyes met mine, his face froze with a curious look.

"Hello," he said in a slow, methodical voice. "I am Doctor Lennon and I am on call."

To which I replied, "Hello, I am Jane and I am not...on call."

After our awkward meeting, meds were prescribed and all was well. I had sprained a tendon in my hand. That was one of those occasions when you have to wear your humor eyes, even though your real eyes are decorated with false eyelashes.

When I became more acquainted with the story of bold and beautiful Esther, I felt honored that someone had compared me to this amazing woman. I claim a kindred spirit to this queen as we all should, since the story of Esther gives us insight into six powerful lessons:[10]

Lesson 1: God has a plan for our lives. It is up to us to find out what our talents are and exploit them in the service of others. What a great reward.

Lesson 2: We are given divine moments to alter circumstances. Pay attention to those events in life that may buckle your knees. Adversity is not your enemy; make it your friend. This may be a moment of divine intervention.

Lesson 3: We must stand with courage. Learn to be brave and daring. Challenge yourself to greater heights; you may be surprised.

Lesson 4: Fasting and prayer bring clarity and hope for deliverance.

Lesson 5: God demands obedience. Read the first few chapters of Genesis.

Lesson 6: God uses everything and everybody for His divine purpose. We live life forward and understand it backward—it is all about trust.

And to complete the list, here's my **Lesson 7:** Was Esther the first-ever beauty queen to actually bring about world peace? Who knows! I can say with confidence that if we take to heart these lessons from the book of Esther, our most challenging flip-flops will eventually sparkle and shine.

ESTHER DID THE HOKEY POKEY

I saw a bumper sticker one time that made a profound impact on me. It simply said, *What if the Hokey Pokey IS what it's all about?*

Think about the words to the song. If you do the right thing, you can shake issues off and then turn things around. Here is an example of how our first beauty queen handled issues:

"You put your right foot in..."
Mordecai said:

"For if you remain silent at this time, relief and deliverance for the Jews will arise from another place, but you and your father's family will perish. And who knows but that you have come to your royal position for such a time as this?" (Esther 4:14)

"Shake it all about..."
Then Esther sent this reply to Mordecai:

"Go and gather together all the Jews of Susa and fast for me. Do not eat or drink for three days, night or day. My maids and I will do the same. And then, though it is against the law, I will go in to see the king. If I must die, I must die." So Mordecai went away and did everything as Esther had ordered him. (Esther 4:15–17)

"Turn yourself around..."
Then Harbona, one of the king's eunuchs, said:

Haman has set up a sharpened pole that stands seventy-five feet tall in his own courtyard. He in-

*tended to use it to impale Mordecai, the man who
saved the king from assassination.*

*"Then impale Haman on it!" the king ordered.
So they impaled Haman on the pole he had set up
for Mordecai, and the king's anger subsided. (Esther 7:9–10)*

We all have had Hokey Pokey moments. It happened
to Thomas and me on a lovely visit to a tropical paradise on a "perk" trip.

Thomas and I had just finished our meal at a lovely
awards banquet. Walking through the beautiful wide
hallway, I noticed a woman approaching us. She was
holding what I later discovered was her glass of
"courage."

Just a bit "overserved," she walked up to Thomas
and said, "You are a horrible person." From that intro,
a rant of colorful words spewed from her mouth.
Thomas and I were dumbfounded by her tone and language. In between her words, I heard something that
stuck with me. She kept repeating, "Eight years ago."
Her anger was related to not being voted to serve on a
council of peers of which Thomas was a member.

Thomas is such a godly man that, when she finished
with her verbal abuse, he simply said, "I am sorry if I
have offended you in any way."

I had to revisit her continued repeating of the phrase,
"Eight years ago." I asked her, "Sugar, you mean you
have been carrying this around for eight years? Don't

you know there are folks who can help you get rid of this?" I actually felt sorry for her.

After a few moments in a less heated conversation, she accepted Thomas's apology and calmed down. I asked her, "Are you okay?"

"Yes," she replied. "Are you a psychologist?"

"No," I responded. "Worse than that. I am a professional speaker. Thank you for the new material."

The story does not end there. Every step I took back to the room, I could feel myself getting angry. Basically, her negative attitude jumped on me. "I cannot believe what just happened! That woman has some nerve talking to you like that!" I exclaimed to Thomas.

With quiet confidence, Thomas simply responded, "Jane, she has a problem. I am not going to let her problem be my problem."

Well, that made me angrier. All aboard! Let's ride on that endless wheel of misfortune.

I did what she did; I refused to let it go. I fired up my laptop and emailed all of my girlfriends. I wasn't finished. I also emailed my children, describing this terrible incident and how Thomas was attacked by this woman...and blah, blah, blah.

In the meantime, Thomas was in bed, ready for a good night's sleep.

I started up again since I wanted to talk it to death. "Is that all you have to say about this?" I asked with a fiery tone.

I will never forget the next thing out of his mouth.

It was the longest, loudest snore I have ever heard. Yes, my sweetie was sound asleep. You know why? He did the Hokey Pokey. Simply put, he did the right thing. He shook it off and turned it around. Yes, indeed. That *is* what it is all about.

Esther was beautiful, she was brave, and she was laser-focused on saving her people. She was wise. She knew when to open her mouth and she knew what to say. An entire book of the Bible is named after her. If you were to have a book named after you, what would the chapters say? Think about it.

Esther's Flip-Flop: With just the right encouragement, her flip-flops became stilettos.

Esther's Sparkle and Shine: Esther is one of two women who have their very own book in the Bible. You go, girl!

How can you shine in the midst of your mess-ups? Develop courage, challenge yourself. Keep focused on the greater good.

Chapter 5

Mother-of-Nations Sarah

God also said to Abraham, "As for Sarai your wife, you are no longer to call her Sarai; her name will be Sarah. I will bless her and will surely give you a son by her. I will bless her so that she will be the mother of nations; kings of peoples will come from her."
(Genesis 17:15–16 NIV)

braham's wife, Sarai, was barren. When a woman could not produce children, it was believed to be a sign that there was something in the woman's life that was causing God not to bless her.[11] This brought anguish, shame, and despair to Sarai.

Don't you know she was talked about for being barren? Don't you know she was talked about for being an old mother? Poor Sarai. We have something in common.

INFERTILITY WITH A FERTILE SENSE OF HUMOR

"Suga," said Dr. Gamewell "Curly" Watson, "I'm gonna give you one year to get pregnant. If you don't get pregnant this year, I'm sending you to a fertility specialist." Ugh. During that year, I thought about Sarai and noticed every tabloid magazine with the caption *Woman Has Litter of Six*.

I am sure every month that went by, Sarai wept over her infertility. I did too. Birthdays were a lovely reminder that *you are not getting any younger, honey*. After one year, just as Curly Watson promised, I found myself in a fertility clinic being treated by a Canadian fertility specialist with a name I could not pronounce. His name was all consonants—Dr. Flfft. I felt stupid saying his name since I pronounced it like a cat would sound when angry. One day, I asked him if he made any money.

"Yes," replied Dr. Flfft.

"Well," I said, "how about buying a vowel?"

I was turned inside out and upside down. One test revealed that I had a blocked fallopian tube. Then Dr. Flfft went after Thomas. Being Canadian, he loved to use the expression *Sendz out Z mounties for Z menz*. Yes, Dr. Flfft was not only intelligent, he had a sense of humor.

The monthly ultrasound was a huge challenge. I was the office infertility champion of timing with a full bladder procedure. I would stop in Trenton, South Carolina, and purchase a Diet Sprite. By the time I got to the doctor's office, my bladder was full, but I had great control. Bless their hearts and bladders, some of the women "lost it" and had to start over.

Finally, praise the Lord, another procedure was perfected with a device that was more personal but much preferred over the full bladder procedure. Dr. Flfft had the task of purchasing cases of condoms. He said the folks he purchased his supplies from thought he was "quite z stud."

During my one year of treatment, Thomas had a procedure as well. The conclusion was that we were finally baby-ready. I have said many times that I know what it is like to wait seven and a half years for the first pregnancy and seven and a half minutes for the second one. Yes, we had a miracle. Sarai did too but not without some drama.

Since Sarai could not produce a child for Abraham, she made a decision that would affect all of humanity. She decided to give Hagar, her Egyptian maid, to Abraham to produce a child. Abraham accepted Sarai's offer to produce a child through Hagar and the result was the birth of Ishmael. However, more than just a child was produced. With the pregnancy, Hagar despised Sarai and Sarai became jealous and harsh with Hagar. Hagar then left and went into the wilderness of Shur.

Sarai decided to "play God" and handle things in her own way. Aren't we all guilty of moving ahead of God's timing? In the middle of this major infertility flip-flop, Sarai used Hagar to provide an heir, Ishmael. Yep,

Sarai created another flip-flop since she became jealous of Hagar and was not very kind.

Pregnant and alone in the wilderness, an angel of the Lord spoke to Hagar. The angel told her to return to Sarai. He also told her that she would bear a son, Ishmael, because God heard her affliction. He said that Ishmael would be a wild man and his hand would be against every man and would one day have many sons and live in the presence of all his brethren in Shur. Ishmael would later become the father of all Arab peoples.[12]

In His perfect timing, God sent Sarai the promise of being the mother of many nations. Her name was changed to Sarah and she bore a son, Isaac. Well, things got somewhat testy as Isaac grew. Ishmael made fun of him. Can you imagine the life Abraham was living? It is bad enough when "momma ain't happy." Abraham had two unhappy mommas under one tent.

Early the next morning Abraham got some food and a bottle of water. The bottle was made out of animal skin. He gave the food and water to Hagar, placing them on her shoulders. Then he sent her away with the boy. She went on her way and wandered in the Desert of Beersheba. When the water in the bottle was gone, she put the boy under a bush. Then she sat down about as far away as a person can shoot an arrow. She thought, "I can't stand to watch the boy die." As she sat there, she began to sob.

God heard the boy crying. Then the angel of God called out to Hagar from heaven. He said to her, "What is the matter, Hagar? Do not be afraid. God has heard the boy crying as he lies there. Lift up the boy and take him by the hand. I will make him into a great nation." (Genesis 21:14–18, NIRV)

God also protected the mother of Ishmael and gave her a promise. Even though Sarah was anxious to do God's work and created a volatile situation, God was faithful to protect and restore both Sarah and Hagar.

Although Sarah initially started out with an empty womb, she became the mother of many nations. This story contains many wonderful lessons. Regardless of our age, we can be used in spite of our weaknesses. As we develop our faith, we also have the ability to affect future generations. What a great reminder for all women.

NURSING NATURES

My dear mother-in-law, Mama Jewell, told me many times that children are born with natures. Just like Ishmael and Isaac, these young men had natures. Isaac's name means "the laughing one."[13] The name *Ishmael* means "God will hear."[14] These names translate perfectly to highlight the humor of Sarah and Abraham having this late-in-life child and the cries of another mother whose child had a flip-flop with destiny.

For countless years, I cried out to God for a child and through it all, I had to develop a sense of humor. When I finally became a mother, I was crying even more; I was clueless.

Holmes is my firstborn. He decided to stay in gestation for nine and a half months. That child just could not bring himself to be born. I think he was playing the video game *Womb Raider*.

I was excited about being a mother and clueless at the same time. What did I really know about babies? So many women told me, "Don't worry. They come with instructions." I think my set of instructions got stuck in my uterus.

I had to have a C-section. Ironically, this was the same section I was placed in when I entered first grade. With the surgical C-section come lots of fluids and pain meds. One tends to swell when pumped full of liquids.

My parents had grandbabies born back-to-back, a day apart. I knew that after being with my sister the day before and traveling to Augusta to see me, they would be very tired and emotional. My mother gingerly peeked in my hospital room, froze in her tracks, and stared at me. "Oh, Momma!" I exclaimed. "I am a mother!"

My always truthful and very tired mother replied, "You look like hell."

The next challenge was nursing. I was determined to give it a go. My mother never nursed her children; she said we "drew blood" like we were some kind of vampire babies.

The breastfeeding book I read said that the most important thing to remember is to be confident. Watching me attempt to feed my newborn, my mother said, "He's going to starve. You have nothing to offer. I've never seen a flat-chested woman feed a baby."

Despite Momma's honest comments, I nursed Holmes for a full year. I actually stopped nursing when he pulled away from me one day, looked at me, and said, "Cracker?" Holmes likes to tell people that he said, "Double-stuffed Oreo?"

As I look back, I realize that my children's natures were revealed during those times of nursing. Holmes was laid back; he did nothing but smile. It was like he wanted to tell me a joke or something he had discovered. And he refused to burp. I even researched how to burp a baby—nothing worked. Now he is great at it.

Caroline was perfectly predictable. She nursed one side, burped on cue, and then nursed on the other side. She was on her own schedule. It was as if she were saying, "I'd like to nurse ten minutes on each side, please. Then I will burp. After this, I will play with my toys in my playpen. After twenty minutes of playing, I will take a 2.4-hour nap."

As adults, Holmes and Caroline are the same way— minus the nursing.

Sarai and Hagar had many moments filled with both laughter and tears; they remind me of what motherhood is all about. As moms, we have all looked to heaven and cried out, "Do you hear me?"

I do think Mama Jewell was correct in believing that children are born prepackaged. We will have numerous flip-flops with them and we will weep with their many mess-ups. This story is also a reminder that through it all, our heavenly father is with us.

STICKY SITUATION

I wonder if Sarah experienced the challenges of being an older mother. When my children entered first grade, some of the younger parents could have technically been my children. Also, I had more facial hair than some of the dads.

Being the older mature mother, I was experienced. Or so I thought. The perky kindergarten teacher gave parents a list of supplies to buy for their child. One of the items on the list was a glue stick. Well, I had a bag of glue sticks—*hot* glue sticks. I proudly presented the teacher with a large bag filled with glue sticks for all the children. She took one look at my bag, halfway grinned, and then, after a long chuckle, said, "I don't think our babies will be using hot glue guns."

I was totally embarrassed but thankfully used my

sense of humor. "Oh, wow! I am sorry your 'babies' are not as advanced as my child."

QUEEN OF THE WORLD

Just for fun, I often said to Caroline, "Who is Momma?"

In her sweet, childlike way, she'd respond, "Momma, you are queen of the world."

"That's right, honey. Momma's got a crown."

It was open house at school. Every detail was in place for the parents to stroll through the lower-grade classrooms. As soon as Thomas and I walked into the room, Caroline excitedly grabbed our hands to show us all of her work and cute drawings. Then I noticed a clothesline hanging across the room with clothespins holding pictures of family portraits drawn by the children. Of course, I could not wait to see what Caroline had drawn. To my horror, she had our family members drawn as tiny stick people. In the background was a massive globe with a big smile and crown on top of the "world"—a picture of me.

Another parent stopped beside me and stared. "Dang," he said. "I wonder who them people are."

Very casually I commented, "Oh, that must be the Joneses."

MOTHERHOOD MISHAPS

I keep telling myself that I am a good mother. I know I tried my best when my children were young—that I know for sure. I have learned a few lessons about motherhood along the way that I'd like to share:

1. If you drive a Suburban or other large vehicle, you will be asked to drive for those lovely outings called field trips. Invest in a smart car instead. Or, if you must drive, ask the teacher to ride with you. The bad kids will ride with you and the teacher, but she will keep them in line.

2. Always have paper towels and baby wipes on hand. Children will throw up. They especially like to get sick in your new car.

3. Do not get involved with school disciplinary matters. Let the teacher handle them. I told my children, "You belong to them during the school hours, but after school hours, you belong to me." You better pray.

4. Do not go to school with a box full of kittens to give away.

5. Don't let your dog in season visit the school with another dog. It annoys the principal, as "no one was amused except the biology class."

6. Do not substitute-teach with a hole in the back of your pants.

7. Do not substitute-teach.

8. Do not make your children drink coffee instead of taking their Ritalin.
9. If you do your child's homework and get a bad grade, do not call the teacher and complain about your grade.
10. Listen to the third-grade teacher when she asks you to stop helping your child with math.
11. Being banned from driving for field trips is not a bad thing because you achieve the status of "cool mom." I talked in federal court when Holmes was in the eleventh grade and had to sit by the teacher. Whatever...

PERKS AND PITFALLS FOR PARENTS

There are perks for older parents—you may have accrued more financial resources and you are somewhat wiser. As an older mother, I have seen parents make some mistakes that can be destructive to families as a child matures.

I do not boast of being the perfect mother nor does Thomas claim to be the ideal father, but I believe that one of the most important lessons we can teach our children is accountability. Some of the most impossible adults to work with are not accountable to authority, and they have a sense of entitlement. Maybe they were spoiled or maybe they have never had a boss to answer to. Everything is fine until you have to correct their behavior; then they will turn on you with a vengeance. The sad part is that these folks are often totally unaware of how to take the blame because they have never been taught accountability. They resort to spinning words or situations to avoid having to take responsibility. Avoid these people as much as the plague.

I have told my children there are two ways to learn lessons in life. You can either listen to the wisdom of people who love and care about you or let the world teach you. The truth is the world can be cruel; most people do not care one bit about you.

As I think of Sarai-turned-Sarah, I realize that God in his wisdom knew when to bless this couple with children. I feel the same way about the timing of my becoming a parent. Unlike Sarah, I am not the mother of many nations. Neither are you. But we should act like we are.

All mothers should pay attention to the words of Ted Harris's song, "The Hand That Rocks the Cradle." The song references a mother's sleepless nights and the cover worn off her Bible. Motherhood and parenthood are not to be taken casually. It is an honor to parent a child and a massive responsibility to set a good example by the way you live. If you want to confuse a child, say one thing and do another.

My parents modeled honesty for me in many ways. Here is one example. When you live on a farm, your income is controlled by weather and market prices. Farming is a risky profession. Since the crop was not profitable my freshman year of college, my parents accepted a government grant. I was automatically given another grant for my sophomore year. But Daddy produced a good crop that year on the farm, and he had more income. My parents decided to send back the check. In my mother's words, "We are giving this money back. Someone else needs a chance to go to college."

I'll never forget that story. My parents probably never knew how much their honest act of kindness and unselfishness impacted me.

RED FLAGS OR BUST

I love my son, Holmes, but rearing this child has been a lesson in patience for Thomas and me. You may identify with this prayer: "Lord, help me help him. Close my big mouth and help me to open my heart to accept the things I cannot change. Help me to trust that you are doing a work in him that I am not privileged to see. But can you please hurry up?! Amen." Or my newest saying, "Lord give me coffee to change the things I can change and wine to accept the things I can't."

At one time, Holmes was out of college, working several low-skill jobs. It was a tough lesson but he learned quickly that an education is an important step toward a fulfilling life and career. It was during this time I was praying hard for Holmes and seeking wisdom on how to help him make his way back to college without enabling. The answer to my prayer came in a most unexpected way.

"Mom!" said my son in a frantic tone. "I was delivering a pizza and this old woman answered the door!"

"Well, what's so bad about that?" I asked.

"Oh, Mom! She was old and wearing a Confederate flag bra," exclaimed Holmes.

The humorist in me kicked in. "Yeah, I bet her bra size was a 38 LONG. And, by the way, that South will never rise again."

The amazing part of this story is that the experience was so disturbing to my child that he reenrolled in college. God comforted me as well as answered my prayers...in the most unusual way.

God also heard the prayers of Sarah and Hagar and comforted the heavy hearts of these biblical women. What a great reminder to those of us whose knees continue to make an indelible mark on the floor as we pray for our children.

Sarah's Flip-Flop: She meddled with God's perfect timing.

Sarah's Sparkle and Shine: She learned to trust God's timing.

How can you shine in the midst of your mess-ups? Meditate on this Scripture that was and still is a huge comfort to me: "But they that wait upon the Lord shall renew their strength; they shall mount up with wings as eagles; they shall run, and not be weary; and they shall walk, and not faint" (Isaiah 40:31 KJV).

Chapter 6

Salty Mrs. Lot

*But Lot's wife looked back, and she
became a pillar of salt.*

(Genesis 19:26 NIV)

FROM RHINESTONES TO BRIMSTONES

Henry David Thoreau once said, "Never look back unless you are planning to go that way." This quote reminds me of Lot's wife, since she did not want to let go of her life in the sinful city of Sodom. So what happens in Sodom stays in Sodom? Not really.

Let it go are three very challenging words. I have heard this little sentence countless times throughout my life. No doubt it is sound advice but also reminds me of another universal truth—one of the few consistent facts in life is change. How we handle change on our ever-spinning wheel of womanhood is the real issue. Not letting go and trusting God's perfect timing can cause major flip-flops and mess-ups. Just read the story of Mrs. Lot and you will discover another sentence with only three words: *Remember Mrs. Lot.*

One of the angels grasped Mrs. Lot's hand (Genesis 19:16). Her hand. Held on tight. Led her away from the sins of her past. Pointed her toward a whole new future. Go this way, Mrs. Lot, and sin no more. She was forced into her new life; she had to look ahead. This is a story of trust and obedience.

> *The first direct reference we have of Lot's un-named wife is when the angels came to hasten the family out of doomed Sodom (Genesis 19:15). Who she was, of what race and family, of what life and character, by what name she was known, the Bible is silent. All the information we have about her is packed into one short verse: "His wife looked back from behind him, and she became a pillar of salt." Yet we must give attention to her for it is written in burning words by the finger of God—"Remember Lot's wife."* [15]

I love the comparison Liz Curtis Higgs makes in her book *Bad Girls of the Bible*, as she identifies Deceived Eve's flip-flop with the same mind-set of Mrs. Lot. Both of these "naughty" gals broke the one commandment given to each of them.

Then she [Mrs. Lot] did the unthinkable. The impermissible. Like Eve, who broke God's single decree, "Don't eat," Mrs. Lot broke the one command given her, "Don't look."

She "looked toward the cities" (NLV), instead of focusing on her future. She "looketh expectingly" (YLT), but in the wrong direction entirely.

Oh, this truth cuts way too close for comfort.[16]

What can we learn from this woman? "I am not like her!" you may say in protest. But have you ever had to leave your comfort zone? I believe Mrs. Lot may justifiably be labeled the salt of the earth because there is a little bit of her in all of us. Many times we look back because we are fearful of what lies in front of us.

I certainly have not lived in an environment like Sodom, but I know how tough it is to leave a place you love. I remember like it was yesterday, having to move from our farm to a new location, only a few miles down the road. But I had to leave my favorite oak tree with my makeshift tree house as well as a sandy dirt hole, wonderful wide ditches, and the rutted road I rode my bike down to visit my grandparents, Lou and Gumpa. These physical places represented comfort and security. In fact, my mother had to literally dig me out of the dirt hole to transport me to my new home. I did look back—no pillar-of-salt moment but definitely tears of salt. There also have been other tough times of moving forward and not wanting to let go.

NEVER SAY NEVER

I frequently begin my speeches with a simple question: Have you ever said, "I will *never* _____, only to eat your words?" I am sure Mrs. Lot thought she would never leave her home either. Sodom was a place where, more than likely, everyone knew her.

I was known in Greenville, South Carolina. After an exciting year of serving our state as Miss South Carolina, I knew the day would come when my life as the queen in this wonderful city would come to an end. That rhinestone crown would be removed from my head and my life would flip-flop to another title: Former Miss South Carolina. But I had found my new home and truly believed I would never leave the city and certainly never live in a small town.

Once I walked into a gift shop and was recognized by the owner, who loaded me up with all kinds of gifts. The dry cleaners would not let me pay for their services; restaurants would comp my meals. I had found my home in a nice, big city. Or so I thought.

Then I met *him*. Yes, him…the man I had prayed for since I was a teenager. *Lord, help me to know him when I meet him*, was my prayer. I had my first encounter with Thomas at the Francis Marion Hotel in Charleston when he introduced me as the newly crowned Miss "Chaleston" (he dropped the *r*). It was so perfectly Southern.

Knowing he judged pageants, I called him to ask if

he would be interested in judging the Miss Charleston Pageant. I wanted to make a great impression, so I acted queenly and mature. Here is how the conversation went:

"Hello," I said.

"Hello," Thomas said.

Then we had some small talk. "What have you been doing?" I asked.

Are you ready for this answer? This is exactly what he said: "Artificially inseminating my beef cattle."

Now, I ask you, what would you say to that answer? Well, my brief encounter with maturity disappeared. I could not help myself. "Really?" I said with a laugh. "What do you do afterward? Smoke a cigarette?" He did not laugh...at all.

Then came the "prayed for" and much anticipated evening when, as Miss South Carolina, I was seated by Thomas at the South Carolina Jaycee banquet. Sparks flew; love was in the air.

One week later, Thomas met me at the Columbia, South Carolina, airport. It had been one whole week since we had met. I just knew he would woo me and take me, The Queen, out to a fabulous restaurant. With flickering candles and beautiful mood music, he would pop the question at a five-star restaurant. Wrong again. He took me out to eat at a "meat and five" called the Lizard's Thicket. This is a family-style restaurant known for their Kountry Cookin'. In between the family-size bowls filled with sweet potatoes and collards, Thomas got romantic.

Later, I asked him what possessed him to pop the question at the Lizard's Thicket. He said that during the meal he got a funny feeling in the pit of his stomach. He thought it was love but later realized it was the collard greens.

LIFE IN A TOWN CALLED IN-BETWEEN

I knew Thomas was a fine man who farmed and had a lovely family, but that is all I knew. After enthusiastically agreeing to be his wife, I asked the most shocking question: "Where do you live?"

Thomas said what I consider to be the worst place in South Carolina—"In-between." I did not hear anything but "in-between," and, like Mrs. Lot, I knew I was in for a big change. "In-between" was a place where I was not known. It was a place I had to trust God, a place where I had to look forward and not look back. I only wish an angel had grabbed my hand and helped lead me.

Thomas and I were married six months later, and I moved to a new town with two lights and with a grand population of 2,500. We lived in the Herlong pond house—a one-thousand-square-foot concrete structure with only two rooms. It was situated on the edge of a pond and a cow pasture. It was not uncommon for me to be awakened by a three-hundred-pound heifer scratching her head on our house.

The little town of Johnston, South Carolina, was a big change for me. I have found that the local folks are fine people, and I have grown to love small-town life. Today, not much has changed except Thomas now works with New York Life. Our town is so small that Thomas shares his office with Bland Funeral Home. I like to refer to the business as New York Life or Death.

Looking forward also means looking for humor, and this town is a treasure. Betty Derrick Bland Dowd is our local funeral home owner and she is an amazing woman. When my aunt Elise Herlong Horne passed away, Betty had to practically conduct a one-woman funeral. I saw her lead the family into the church, properly seat them, and then jump into action when the pianist did a no-show. Betty sat down at the piano and played beautiful sacred hymns and Aunt Elise's favorite songs. After the last song, Betty got right back into funeral mode and led the family out of the church and to the cemetery. The only thing she did not do that day was fill in the grave.

A friend of mine told me about the funeral of a lovely stepmother with a beautiful blended family. The stepdaughter forgot to cut her phone off during the service. As the lid of the casket was raised for the final viewing, the stepdaughter's ringtone blared throughout the church. The congregation heard her favorite song from her favorite musical, *The Wizard of Oz*: "Ding-dong, the witch is dead. Which old witch? The wicked witch. Ding-dong the wicked witch is dead."[17]

Can you imagine? During the most reverent moment of the service, that song rang through the church. One of her family members went to console her at the burial after the embarrassing incident. "Are you okay?" he asked.

Her response was a classic moment of finding humor. She replied, "If I only had a brain."[18]

Maybe Mrs. Lot would have benefited from using her brain to avoid the temptation of looking back during her emotional moment. The story of Lot's wife is only one verse in Genesis. It is paired with a powerful warning in the New Testament: "Remember Lot's wife" (Luke 17:32). Why should we remember her? Simply put, we should strive for a life that is sparkling with rhinestones, not a life ending with fire and brimstone.

A "LOT" OF CHANGE

Have you ever wondered what would have happened if Lot's wife trusted what God was doing and did not look back? Maybe she could have become a rock-star pillar in her new community instead of a pillar of salt. We will never know, but I do know that trusting God while crying salty tears is challenging.

It was the dead of summer. One of the first things I did every morning was open the shutters and look at the soybean field after pleading with God for rain.

Thomas was farming and had planted a beautiful crop of soybeans. The poor little sprouts were struggling and literally dying of thirst. In addition, the drought was affecting our cattle; the once lush green hue of the hay fields had changed into a depressed shade of brown.

We had had no rain for weeks. Thomas and I prayed and trusted God but we did not like His answer. South Carolina was in a state of emergency and we were in a state of spiritual confusion.

During this time, Thomas discovered a profound revelation. There was no spiritual help or resource for farmers who experience the pain of loss. Thomas called several friends involved in agriculture, and from those conversations the Fellowship of Christian Farmers was born. The "office" was located in our basement and grew into an international organization that was moved to Illinois.

Today the organization is still growing strong.[19] Fellowship of Christian Farmers International (FCFI) celebrated its twenty-fifth anniversary last year, and the impact this organization has had in our country and across the world is simply amazing. Last year alone, the FCFI shared the gospel with over 250,000 people by telling the story of salvation using a string of beads and a walking stick. If you multiply this with the influence of FCFI over a twenty-five-year period, the numbers are astounding.[20]

Thomas has celebrated many personal successes in life, but if you ask him the achievement he is the most proud of, it would be his work organizing the Fellowship of Christian Farmers International.

If your goal is to move from adversity to abundance, then trust God, move forward, and don't look back.

Mrs. Lot's Flip-Flop: She did not want to let go of her former life and look ahead. She longed for her past.

Mrs. Lot's Sparkle and Shine: Brimstone.

How can you shine in the midst of your mess-ups? Trust that God is pointing you to a new direction—he's got your back but try not to look back.

Chapter 7

Dynamic Duo Naomi and Ruth

*"Don't call me Naomi," she told
them. "Call me Mara, because the
Almighty has made my life very bitter.
I went away full, but the Lord has
brought me back empty."*
(Ruth 1:20–21a NIV)

The book of Ruth is loaded with a myriad of flip-flops. The overriding theme is change and how it can affect us. It is also a book that addresses loss, devotion, new beginnings, and a humongous pity party.

WAS NAOMI A WHINER?

"I'm hearing lots of whine; where's the cheese?" I will never forget this one-liner. My family was on vacation in Litchfield Beach, South Carolina, and heard this statement from some "Nath'ners" who were correcting their children. Normally when you think about wine and cheese, it represents some sort of celebration. This whiny story reminds me of poor Naomi since, at one time, she had nothing to celebrate.

Naomi had lost her husband and two sons. She was probably hitting menopause, having hot flashes—also known as personal summers or power surges. Be honest. We have all either known a Naomi, been a Naomi, or both.

I am going to admit my worst Naomi Moment. I was in the thick of a horrible family problem. I was shocked, bewildered, and just plain pathetic. The event coincided with caring for my mother-in-law, who was suffering from dementia. Every morning I was responsible for preparing breakfast for Mama Jewell and making sure she was taking her medicines before the arrival of her caretaker.

As we sat at the round oak table, Mama Jewell's face glowed with kindness and consideration. She began our conversation, as sweet as ever. "Honey, how are you doing?"

"Oh, Mama Jewell. Did I tell you about my family problem?" I inquired.

"Why, no, da'lin'! Is something wrong?"

"Oh, yes." Then I hopped on my pitiful wheel of misfortune. After a fifteen-minute ride of sorrow, worry, and fears, I watched Mama Jewell's eyes glisten with heartfelt compassion.

The conversation lulled, then started up again. "Honey, how are you doing?"

"Oh, Mama Jewell. Did I tell you about my family problem?" I asked.

"Why, no, da'lin! Is something wrong?"

"Oh, yes," I repeated. It was my second ride on that endless wheel since Mama Jewell was having trouble with her short-term memory. Part of me enjoyed talking about it...again. And again.

I was using my precious mother-in-law's memory issues to hear myself talk about my problem over and over again. Then it hit me: Mama Jewell is not nearly as sick as I am!

My Naomi Moment reminded me that I had totally lost my sparkle. I had allowed events to make me a dull human being. That episode led me to seek the help of a professional counselor who had The Counselor living in his heart. I learned healthy skills for dealing with impossible people.

Will you challenge yourself to do the same? If not, find a memory ward at the nearest nursing home and go find someone to listen to your story like I did, over and over again. The residents will love your company, and you will get to hear yourself whine over and over.

Charles R. Swindoll writes in his book *The Grace Awakening*, "I am convinced that life is 10% what happens to me and 90% how I react to it. We cannot change our past...we cannot change the fact that people will act in a certain way."[21]

So, the *h* was eventually dropped in my old whine and new wine was put into my new "wineskin" (Luke 5:37–39 NKJV). Now, that is something to celebrate.

NEED A GOOD GLEANING?

Please understand that I am not being insensitive to Naomi. She knew grief after losing her husband and both of her sons.[22] Many have faced unbelievable grief that may seem insurmountable. The good news is that there are professionals who can help with grief. After losing both my mother and sister within a five-month period, it was a godsend to seek professional help. I only wish I had visited this wonderful counselor sooner.

There was a time when I felt nothing but warm tears running down my face. Part of me was gone and I would never be the same. Thank the Lord someone recommended the book *Life After Loss: A Practical Guide to Renewing Your Life After Experiencing Major Loss,* by Bob Deits. I was on auto-pilot reading that book until I saw a letter that Deits had included written by a grieving woman. It totally spoke to my heart; I could have easily written that letter.

I hate grief: it hurts your heart and consumes your mind. I will never forget when one of my best buds lost her husband in a tragic plane crash. I called her almost every day and would ask the same question: "How are you?" Her answers were the same until one day she said, "I am better. I did not think of Charles today for five minutes." Her answer stunned me and I realized the enormous pain Mary was experiencing. Now it was my turn.

When I read the grieving woman's letter I realized that grief is a terrible emotion to experience but a necessary step in the healing process. *Life After Loss* helped me to understand this is an experience we must go through to get through. What really spoke to my heart was that the woman wrote the letter to Grief and wisely answered her own letter from Grief. It was a turning point for me when Grief apologized and identified with my raw feelings and broken heart. I gained skills to deal with this painful flip-flop and saw the tremendous value for my own healing in embracing grief. Deits added this wonderful comment after the letter: "She is again a person with a zest for living and an energy level that *sparkles.*"[23]

I promise, I did not add that last word. How about that! Naomi could have used this wonderful suggestion to handle her grief in a heathier way. I am telling you the truth: if you get the right help, you will restore your energy and rediscover your shine.

Now, in Naomi's case, God is so good. Talk about grace!

Naomi had not only experienced utter ruin, but found her identity in the tragic state of her existence. And yet, God used Naomi to graft Ruth into the lineage of Jesus Christ.[24]

PITY PARTIES DON'T SPARKLE AND SHINE

I engaged in my own personal pity party, soap opera I call "As the My World Flops." Have you ever had a similar party? Let me share a word of warning that pity parties have no beautifully wrapped gifts and there is only one guest—you. I imagine since Naomi's world was turned upside down, she had many moments of self-pity.

Being pitiful is tolerated by folks for just so long. After a while, some may screen your calls using caller ID and autotext to avoid hearing the same story over and over. If you continue to wallow in your own pity, you are lucky to receive a sad-face emoji on your smartphone. When this starts to happen, you better get your act together.

Regardless of how much you lean on your dearest friends for comfort, there will come a time when you have got to move on. Your friends will love you, listen to you, and try to help you as much as humanly possible, but your job is to seek solutions to handle your situation and return to a healthy mental state.

I lived with a horrible family situation that I allowed to consume me. I leaned on my buddies to help me, but when Dixie, one of my BFFs, answered her phone, "Now what?" instead of "Hello," I knew it was time to get with it and get over it.

Naomi had a choice, as we all do, on how to define her life moving forward. Instead of Naomi being defined by her "bitter" circumstances, she took control of her circumstances and became "better." Notice the difference between the two words? It is the "I"...it's all about ME. Maybe Naomi's name should be spelled *Naome*.

BE POSITIVE

Clearly, there was a time when Naomi was not feeling too positive about her circumstances. We have all been in a place where there is nothing positive to cling to. Our minds are powerful and our thoughts can be surprising. This next story says so much about how we see things.

One of my Sunday school buds told our class a story I will never forget. As a seventeen-year-old, Nicky entered boot camp. He said that he was petrified and had a sinking feeling of failure. He dropped to his knees and prayed, "Lord, I need help. Please send me a sign to help me survive basic training." With bowed head, Nicky's eyes opened. It was a miracle. He saw his divine answer. Imprinted on his dog tags was *B-Positive*. His entire attitude changed from that moment. God had answered his prayer.

A few days later, a buddy commented on Nicky's change. "What happened to you?" inquired his friend.

Nicky said, "My fears are gone. I got a message from God. Look at my dog tags, B-Positive."

"Really?" commented Nicky's friend. He pulled the long chain out of his shirt and showed Nicky his dog tag. "Look at my message from God—*O-Negative*."

Nicky had no idea that it was his blood type written on his dog tag. But he changed his attitude when he changed his thinking. What a great lesson for all of us.

JUST PLANE PANIC

When faced with loss and uncertainty, many will panic. I don't believe God is the author of the fear and panic. I hate it when my mind starts to race and I fabricate unhealthy thoughts laced with fear. It is a struggle to balance emotions and not think the worst. Ever been there?

I was speaking for several days in south Georgia at one of my favorite events—the Sunbelt Ag Expo. For one week, the Farm Credit folks hauled me around on a flatbed trailer, like an old heifer, to sing and entertain the masses.

I booked a speaking engagement the day after the Sunbelt Expo ended and had to drive to Macon, Georgia, to catch my connecting flight to Atlanta. I was in a panic as I exited the interstate to the Middle Georgia Regional Airport. I kept looking in the sky trying to spot a plane. There were no planes to be seen, and I was getting more panicked by the minute. Even the OnStar advisor was getting miffed with me. They were constantly reassuring me that the airport was only a few minutes away.

Finally, I saw the airfield, but all the airplanes were parked. It was a strange sight. I hurriedly ran into the terminal to the airline counter. The clerk was looking down, cutting his nails with a fingernail clipper. I cleared my throat to get the attention of the gate agent. "Where is the flight to Atlanta?" I asked. "Did I miss it?"

"No, ma'am," replied the gate agent. "We ain't running that plane today."

"What?" I asked. I could not believe my ears. "How am I supposed to get to my connecting flight in Atlanta?"

"The bus," he calmly replied.

Suddenly, I heard the sounds of a large bus making its way into the airport. Behind me sat about fifty other folks who were steaming mad. *Oh boy,* I thought. *This is gonna be pleasant.*

One by one we lined up single file, like kids going on a field trip. Many were talking on their cell phones complaining about this awful turn of events and how they were going to let the airline know about this horrible bus ride.

The driver greeted us with a smile and a cold beverage. Actually, I felt sorry for him; he had a busload of angry travelers.

As soon as we were all seated, the driver made some entertaining comments. "At this time, make sure your seat backs and tray tables are in their full upright position and that your seat belt is correctly fastened. Also, your portable electronic devices must be set to 'airplane' mode until an announcement is made upon arrival. Thank you."

Many of my fellow passengers had the same strange look on their faces as I did. He was talking as if we were on a commercial airplane.

"Do I have your attention yet?" he asked. "By the way, we have no emergency drills or oxygen masks. Seat belts are preferred but optional. There is no exit row, and you can turn on your devices and keep them on. Also, I have provided some delicious drinks and snacks. You can get up anytime you want; plus we have a fine restroom in the back of the bus. The best news is that I know so many shortcuts to Atlanta that you will have time to enjoy a meal and walk leisurely to your connecting flight." To add to the fun, he teased us by singing the first line of the song "A Thousand Bottles of Beer on the Wall."

My panicked attitude changed. I wasn't the only one. Most of the fifty men and women in the bus sat back, relaxed, and enjoyed the ride. When we "landed" in Atlanta, I was amazed how many passengers requested a bus ride back to Macon. They were not interested in flying.

I wasted time and energy thinking the worst. That bus ride turned out to be a delightful experience with a driver who had a positive, contagious attitude. It was a flip-flop that turned into a ride that I will never forget.

> *"Common sense and a sense of humor are the same thing, moving at different speeds. A sense of humor is just common sense, dancing."*
>
> Clive James

STEEL LILIES

Think about the movie *Steel Magnolias*. That movie highlights the love and dedication of strong women and the unbreakable bonds of friendship. Can you imagine if Naomi, Ruth, and Orpah were featured in a movie? I would call it *Steel Lilies*. The movie would open with a mother's prejudice toward Moabite women and her disapproval of her sons' decisions to marry Moabite women. "The Mosaic Law [Deuteronomy 7:3–4] warned the Israelites not to let their sons and daughters marry foreigners, for fear that God's people would be led into idolatry."[25]

How Naomi handled her bias and the tragic events that followed are recorded in the first chapter of the book of Ruth.

Here is the movie trailer:

Meet Naomi, Orpah, and Ruth. We will take an amazing journey with these three Steel Lily ladies.

Tragedy strikes this family with the loss of Naomi's husband and her two sons. We will discover how Naomi embraced her daughters-in-law and why Orpah chose another path. This is a story about death, a journey to another land, dedication, reputation, and, of course, romance.

This movie would be the ultimate chick flick.

I am taken with Ruth. Naomi was heartbroken; sensitive and loyal Ruth stayed with her and traveled to a new land. Ruth also loved and trusted her mother-in-law and listened to her advice on how to capture the attention of Boaz. She married him and gave birth to a son named Obed, who became the grandfather of King David (Ruth 4:17).

There had to be some drama when Ruth traveled with Naomi to Bethlehem.[26] With all that Naomi had to deal with, the "Sisteran" welcomed Naomi. Faithful and loving Ruth stayed with her mother-in-law. When they arrived in Bethlehem, the whole town was stirred because of them (Ruth 1:19). I hope they saw Ruth's pure heart and dedication to Naomi. You have to wonder if certain women—those I call "church ladies"—were skeptical of Ruth, who was not a hometown girl. Our heroine, as one writer puts it, "is a non-Jew and a foreigner, but she still manages to be a shining example of goodness and faith in this crazy world."[27]

Ruth is a lot like Esther, in that both their stories are about a resourceful woman whose courage, loyalty, and faithfulness lead her to a happy ending. Though Ruth lives in a society where men were top dog and women had very few choices, she uses her grace, charm, and, sometimes, wit to get what she wants.[28] *Now that's a female role model.*[29]

You have to wonder what the church ladies thought of Ruth. She was different, so she did not exactly fit in at the beginning.

Church ladies (CLs) scare me. If the Pharisees and the Sadducees had been women, they would fit the profile of a church lady. The best way to explain these folks is that they are "so heavenly minded, that many times, they are no earthly good." And my addendum—they can create a "mell of a hess."

Remember Dana Carvey's character the Church Lady on the early years of *Saturday Night Live*? So many of my minister friends confided in me that they could not wait to watch the segment called "Church Chat." It was quite entertaining and concluded with the infamous line, "Well isn't that special?" Most folks in church leadership thought that skit contained a lot of truth.[30]

Thomas and I traveled for years and shared our faith in just about every denomination. I have met CLs in community fellowships, Pentecostal holiness churches, and mainline denominations. These women are large and in charge. Unfortunately, Thomas and I have seen many church ladies in action. Sadly, they can kill the Spirit and drive many people away from the fellowship. Here are some of my favorite CL lines that I have heard through the years:

"Well, you know _____ is not coming to church. I am gonna say something. That family should *make* them come to church." Yeah, that works.

"I have a prayer request. You know that no-good husband was with that other woman. I saw them..." Hmm. Prayer request—or gossip?

I could go on with this, but in all fairness, there are also many wonderful ladies in churches. I appreciate their love, faithfulness, and service.

One of the most interesting CLs I ever met wore her rhinestone Jesus pin and had a Christian fish on the back of her car. Then after church, she broke in line at the buffet and talked about the church people.

In honor of this unique bunch, I thought it would be fun to rewrite the words to Glen Campbell's song "Rhinestone Cowboy." I call my version "She Wore Her Rhinestone Jesus."

She's been talkin' 'bout the Lord so long
Singin' "I surrender all"
She knows every fault and dirty thoughts of their
*   bad ways.*
Does St. Peter know her name?

Good works make her insane; there are many others to shame

There's been a load of compromisin'
On the road to heaven's horizon
But she's gonna be your light, on bended knee.

She wore her rhinestone Jesus
Walkin' up to the stage like a star-studded holy boast.
She wore a rhinestone Jesus
Rather be saved by the clergy on the radio
Salvation's just part of the show

Well, I joined in the Sunday meal
Their faith seemed to be so real
But the wait at the Sizzler buffet, was such a long stay
She shoved and cut in line
Leaving her flock behind
'Cause she loved chicken piled high
There's been a load of compromisin'
On the road to heaven's horizon
But she's gonna be your light for all to see.

She wore her rhinestone Jesus.
In church she was a saint
But the world saw a different face
She wore a rhinestone Jesus...

*Sending cards and letters to people she doesn't
    even know
Salvation's just part of the show*

This next story is a stinger. I wonder how many folks
we have turned off or away in our own churches?

Gandhi decided he would visit one of the Christian
churches in Calcutta, India. Upon seeking entrance to
the church sanctuary, he was stopped at the door by the
ushers.

He was told he was not welcome, nor would he be
permitted to attend this particular church, as it was for
high-caste Indians and whites only. He was neither high
caste nor white. Because of the rejection, the Mahatma
turned his back on Christianity.

With this act, Gandhi rejected the Christian faith,
never again to consider the claims of Christ. He was
turned off by the sin of segregation practiced by the
church. It was because of this experience that Gandhi
later declared, "I'd be a Christian if it were not for the
Christians."[31]

Here is the warning: be certain your faith walk and talk
line up with God's Word. Many eyes are on you, and on
me, as we live life every day. We do want to sparkle and
shine, but develop your shine from inside out. Also be
aware that some well-meaning church folks will hurt you.
It is up to you to meditate on all things that are good, positive, and pure. Yes, get over those hurts fast.

God can use you. He can use all who seek to improve

themselves and live successfully. Yes, we have failures too. I know that many struggle with reading and believing the Bible, but its wisdom and sound teachings will help all of us find our shine. Yes, issues dull us from time to time, but in my opinion, the Bible is the greatest success book ever written. It also gives us permission to make mistakes and offers the how-tos to fix our mess-ups.

Just like Naomi, we all have our own journeys to travel. It is up to us to find the right people to lean on and look to as well as to gain the wisdom to know the difference. Ruth encouraged Naomi and Naomi encouraged her daughter-in-law, Ruth. Also, maybe Naomi was trying to make sense out of her sorrow. Can you make your pain someone else's gain?

One of the most powerful prayers is the Serenity Prayer, attributed to Reinhold Niebuhr (1892–1971).[32] The first four lines are the most celebrated, but the entire prayer is beautiful. Read this prayer with Naomi and Ruth in mind:

God grant me the serenity
To accept the things I cannot change;
Courage to change the things I can;
And wisdom to know the difference.

Living one day at a time;
Enjoying one moment at a time;
Accepting hardships as the pathway to peace;
Taking, as He did, this sinful world

As it is, not as I would have it;
Trusting that He will make all things right
If I surrender to His Will;
So that I may be reasonably happy in this life
And supremely happy with Him
Forever and ever in the next.
Amen.

DO BLACK DOTS MATTER?

I read a story about a professor who challenged his students with a surprise test. I believe this may have been one of the most important lessons they will ever learn or this wise professor could teach his students. It is all about our focus and the "black dots" in life.

You can imagine everyone's surprise when they saw the test. There were no questions—only a black dot in the center of a white sheet of paper. The professor gave one simple instruction—write about what you see. Every single student, without exception, wrote and attempted to define the one black dot.

The classroom was silent. After all essays had been read, the professor explained why he had given them the test. "I'm not going to grade you on this. I just wanted to give you something to think about. No one wrote about the white part of the paper. Everyone focused on the black dot. The same thing happens in our lives. We have a white piece of paper to observe and enjoy, but we always focus on the dark spots.

"Our life is a gift given to us by God, with love and care, and we always have reasons to celebrate—nature renewing itself every day, our friends around us, the job that provides our livelihood, the miracles we see every day...

"However, we insist on focusing only on the dark spot—the health issues that bother us, the lack of money, the complicated relationship with a family member, the disappointment with a friend. The dark spots are very small when compared to everything we have in our lives, but they're the ones that pollute our mind."[33]

To move into a new life, Naomi had to spend less time focusing on the black dot. So do we. The only way we can truly find happiness and live a life filled with peace is to focus on our blessings.

BACKWARD THOUGHTS GOING FORWARD

You will be inspired by the wisdom in this writing. How do you look at your life?

Today was absolutely the worst day ever.
And don't try to convince me that

There is something good in every day.
Because when you take a closer look,
This world is a pretty evil place.
Even if
Some goodness does shine through once in a while
Satisfaction and happiness don't last.
And it's not true that
It's all in the mind and heart
Because true happiness can be obtained
Only if one's surroundings are good
It's not true that good exists
I am sure you can agree
That
Reality creates my attitude
It's all beyond my control
And you will never in a million years hear me say
Today was a good day
Now, read it backwards[34]
by Chanie Gorkin

HAPPY "TAUGHTS"

My daughter, Caroline, loved watching *Peter Pan* when she was a little girl. She was glued to the television and loved every minute of the animated movie. After watching the movie, she pretended to fly around the house just like Peter Pan.

On one occasion, I was upset over something, and

my sweet Caroline, always a tender child, was very sensitive to my feelings. Her sweet face turned toward mine and her big brown eyes looked at me. She said, "Momma, tink happy taughts. Momma! Tink happy taughts!" she repeated. Then she said something I will never forget: "Momma, if you tink happy taughts, den you will fly like Peter Pan!"

My sweet little toddler was giving me her solution to handling problems. Caroline understood that Peter Pan could fly when he thought about happy things.

Caroline reminded me that if we think positive thoughts, we can soar above our troubles. We will see difficult issues from another viewpoint and handle life's challenges with a different perspective. Happy thoughts will give us altitude for a new attitude.

Finally brothers, whatever is true, whatever is honorable, whatever is right, whatever is pure, whatever is lovely, whatever is admirable—if any excellence and if any worthy of praise—think on these things. (Philippians 4:8 BLB)

When I read this verse of Scripture, it reminds me of the importance of redirecting our thoughts. Like Naomi, we can all think unhealthy thoughts and cry a bucket of tears. How can God communicate and encourage us if we continue to meditate on unhealthy thoughts?

James Altucher is what I call an Internet philosopher. He wrote a wonderful article titled "The Power of

Five."[35] The entire article is full of wisdom but I was impressed with bullet point number three since it has Naomi's name written all over it. Yep, my name is there too. James Altucher sets up his point with an honest confession of his own battles:

> *Sometimes I feel like I'm engulfed in red flames. I don't want to be afraid or anxious any more. There are two banks to the river: on one bank are all the regrets, guilt...past. On the other bank are all the worries, anxieties...future.*
>
> *I lived most of my life on the bottom of the river, clinging to my fears of being swept up by all the currents. It's hard to let go. I was afraid to crash into the banks. Everyone else around me was scared also.*
>
> *But the only way to get to the ocean is by letting go of the fears and anxieties. By not clinging to what was stolen so you can enjoy the energy that is yours forever.*
>
> *I know it's easier said than done, **but this helps me. I hope it helps you too...***
>
> **3) My thoughts are the average of the five things I think about.** *I try for it to be gratitude, abundance, health, value, and WOW! In reverse order.*

Wow, is right. This addresses issues that so many of us deal with. I am thankful that the book of Ruth gives us insight into Naomi's heartaches and gives us permission to be godly women who, at times, struggle with fear and anxiety.

WAS NAOMI A FLASHER?

You do the math. Naomi may have been experiencing the Change. I have heard older women commenting on other women saying, "She's not right, and it may be because of the Change. I thought, *I wonder what they are changing into. Certainly not some sort of uncontrollable person who says whatever, whenever? I will never act like that.*

Other names for these lovely "hot" moments are "private tropical vacations" and your inner child "playing with matches."[36]

Ruth 1:12–13 may give us a hint of menopausal Naomi. In verse 12 she says, "Return, my daughters! Go, for I am too old to have a husband. If I said I have hope, if I should even have..." (NASB). If you are past childbearing years, you may want to throw some confetti, but deep inside that small voice may say, "You are officially old." Then your hormones decide to flip-flop; God help those who are in our path.

I have a friend who had quite an experience when she was going through the Change, more specifically, hot flashes. She overheard her husband ask the children, "Where is your momma?"

One of her children replied, "Daddy, she's in the freezer...again."

Her husband walked into the kitchen and saw an open freezer door with her head shoved inside. "Honey," he said. "Are you cooking?"

"I'm cooking all right," exclaimed my friend. "But it's not dinner."

I know that freezer trick. My head has been in there too.

My friend went on to say that her husband, who worked at the local hospital, told her to come to the emergency room. He had figured out a way to help her with her problem. She was under the impression that her hubby had found a doctor to prescribe some medication. To her shock, he led her to the hospital morgue. "If you sit in here for a few minutes, you will cool right off," he said.

"Well," she told me later, "it worked. I decided that if somebody questioned me about sitting in that morgue, I was gonna tell them that I was paying my respects...to my dead hormones."

THE REASON FOR YOUR FAT

Naomi was probably middle-aged, and that is when the middle starts to shift and emotions start to fly. More than likely, she had a few "fat days," and she searched her wardrobe for the right fat outfit. Nobody likes to wear fat clothes. Many modern-day women have discovered Spanx, but that garment can only stretch so much. Nothing can flip your day faster than digging through your closet searching for fat pants.

Have you ever worn Spanx? Have you ever had a blowout in your Spanx? At first, you may think it is some sort of growth, but on closer inspection, it is your fat. As a female comedian, here is how I see it: trying to stuff fat back into your Spanx is like attempting to reload a can of Pillsbury crescent rolls, or as we refer to them in the South, "whop biscuits." (*Whop* is the sound made when you hit the cylinder on the countertop.)

The older we become, the more we fight the battle of the blowouts. I was in the best shape of my life when I had to parade across the stage at the Miss America Pageant wearing a swimsuit, high heels, and a smile. Walking in front of millions on national television, I was motivated! But I need practical advice. What is a woman to do who struggles to be in control of her weight?

Margaret Marshall has written a book titled *Healthy Living Means Living Healthy: Lose Weight, Feel Great.* Marshall believes "it is not dependent on the numbers on a scale, but rather on how you conduct your thoughts and feelings, and how you manage the many challenges throughout the years."[37]

The cool part about this book is that Marshall includes "weight a minute quotes" at the beginning of every chapter. Here are a few:

1. When you nourish your body, you nourish your mind.
2. Focus is where your attention is and too often your focus is on the immediate, rather than the goal.
3. Some days are more challenging than others, and junk food will always deprive you of your best.
4. Old habits return in weak moments.
5. The starting point for everything in your life is self-care. [38]

I appreciate practical tools and insights to improve every aspect of life—relationships, environment, and level of success. So maybe instead of investing in a pair of Spanx for a temporary victory with fighting fat, every middle-aged woman should check out a program or resource to help balance emotions. Fighting the battle of the bulge starts with a healthy mind and attitude.

I'm going to be honest with you. A really good day for me is when I wake up rested, my hair obeys, my nails are cared for, and my house is clean. I feel good about myself and I can sense my confidence shine. I also want my husband to smile when I make an effort to look my best. This is when I tell the world...watch out; here I come!"

MED: THE TRIPLE FLIP-FLOP

What is MED, aka the Triple Flip-Flop? It is a combination of being hit with three issues at the same time:

menopause, empty nest, and death, or dealing with aging parents. With the loss of her husband and two sons and the probability of menopause, more than likely Naomi dealt with the dreaded **Triple Flip-Flop.** Have you been there? I will never forget when it hit me.

I walked into my empty home; my knees buckled and I hit the floor. I could not stop crying. Both my children were in college, my mother had died only a month before, and my hormones were flipping out.

Thomas was on the riding lawn mower cutting the grass in the dark.

We all grieve in different ways.

Mothers spend years and years dedicating their time and energy to their children. Then it ends. Our children are either absent physically or mentally. It is o-v-e-r. In the meantime, we cannot sleep, our middles are thickening like gravy, and we feel like sweltering beasts in the dead of winter. We spend time with our heads shoved into a freezer and watch hottie grandmother Marie Osmond tell us she lost fifty pounds.

What is the answer to our massive triple flip-flop? Look at John 5:5–9 (BSB).

> *One man there had been an invalid for thirty-eight years. Jesus saw him lying there and realized he had already been there a long time. "Do you want to get well?" he asked.*
>
> *"Sir," replied the sick man, "I have no one to help me into the pool when the water is stirred. While*

I am on my way, someone else goes in before me."
Then Jesus told him, "Get up, pick up your mat,
and walk." Immediately the man was made well,
and he picked up his mat and began to walk.

Yep, there is our answer. Get up, then get out and do something. Do not let MED wreck your emotions. Start early with an interest or hobby that excites you. I am thankful to have a speaking and writing career that I poured myself into after my mother died and my children left. Another interest or something to occupy you when you face overwhelming sadness will make you a healthier person.

I loved my grandmother on my mother's side, but she "celebrated" anniversaries of my grandfather's death and non-birthdays. I can still hear her soft voice that was laced with a sad overtone. She'd say something like, "You know your grandfather would be ninety-eight years old today..." Bless her sweet heart; it just made me sad to hear her dwell on the past and not cultivate another interest. Actually it taught me a lesson—do not become consumed with a spirit of grief.

Be prepared for the triple flip-flop and fight it with prayer and wisdom. You may seek to volunteer your time for a cause or maybe you have a dream that has been buried over the years. Resurrect that dream and make it come true. There is also great literature and medical information to help women with those lovely hormonal issues.

Prepare for the possible triple flip-flop and cull the dull. Be determined to let your light shine brighter than ever. Naomi wisely moved ahead to a new life. God restored her loss and blessed her with the ultimate gift—an heir in the lineage of Jesus Christ.

FIELD OF DREAMS

After the loss of her husband and sons, Naomi may have lost her dreams. The good news is that her loyal daughter-in-law Ruth stayed with her. Eventually Ruth married Boaz and gave birth to a son who was an ancestor of Jesus Christ (Matthew 1:5). God restored double for Naomi's trouble.

When I retrace the steps of Naomi and Ruth, what catches my eye is the significance of the wheat field. The wheat field was a central place where Naomi's dreams were reborn and Ruth's future changed.

I can identify with the work in the field since it was in a hot Johns Island tomato field where I learned many of the same lessons mentioned in the book of Ruth—hard work, consistency, and humility.

First, I learned the value of working hard. In the Bible, Ruth 2:7 says that Ruth gathered the sheaves after the reaper. I am sure there was not much left to glean. I picked the leftover tomatoes after the main crop was harvested three times. That was tough.

Early in the morning, I dragged myself out of bed to

fill my tomato orders to beat the heat. As soon as the dew was dry on the tomato stems, I picked as many tomatoes as possible. To fill the remaining orders, I crawled around in 1,000-pound wooden crates and rescued the tomatoes that would be culled at the shed. Whether I was working on the truck or in the field itself, the work was hard. Each day I mentally prepared myself for long hours of hot, demanding work.

Ruth set herself to the hard work of gathering what the harvesters had missed. I call this extra-mile thinking. What can I do that others are not willing to do? After I picked the tomatoes, I took the fruit to my home and washed off all the fertilizer, dirt, and leaves. This made the fruit look shiny and delicious. I did not have to go to all that trouble, but I discovered folks appreciate attention to detail.

The next quality I notice in Ruth is consistency. Successful people are reliable and persistent. I learned this lesson when I delivered my orders. There was one man who was very hard to please. I thought if I put the best tomatoes on top of each box, he would buy all the boxes. Did he surprise me! He did not care what the tomatoes looked like on the top; he wanted to see the last tomato on the very bottom. Just like that bucket of tomatoes, people stay successful when they are consistent in both their personal (bottom of the box) and professional (top of the box) lives.

Ruth had no sense of entitlement, no expectations of fair and equal treatment. She was not too proud to work in the wheat field. I had worked so hard over several years in the tomato fields that Daddy decided to reward me with the chance to study music and art in Europe for six weeks. Toward the end of my trip, I was in Paris. Standing on top of the Eiffel Tower in awe of the view, I said, "Well, I am standing on top of the Eiffel Tower, but one week from today, I will be leaning over, picking tomatoes."

I was right. I was not too proud to go back to those hot tomato fields. After all, that job got me to the top of the Eiffel Tower, on the Dean's List in college, down a runway of the Miss America Pageant, and the list goes on.

Ruth's simple work in that wheat field was a life-changer since she ultimately grabbed the attention of Boaz. Naomi's life also was forever changed. Many times it is in the common events in life where amazing lessons are learned and where God can do His greatest work. God restored the lives of this dynamic duo, Naomi and Ruth. He can restore yours too.

RHINESTONES ON MY FINGERNAILS

I hope Naomi had girlfriends to help her through her dark moments of loss. Many of us have even had angels come to us who had no idea they were saving us from ourselves. I had my angels too.

They came to my aid in a place called Nail Delights.

This wonderful salon was filled with beautiful Vietnamese women. They were my angels. Once a week, I made my way to a nearby mall to get away from my problems, but it turned into much more than getting a manicure and pedicure. I was experiencing one of the darkest times of my life with my mother's failing health combined with a heartbreaking family lawsuit. These ladies gave me some much-needed treatment for my troubles.

My Nail Delight ladies had the most unusual names: Ha, Mee, and Thumb. With big smiles and even bigger hearts, they asked, "Jane, how you doin'?" Week after week, I shared my heartache with them, and they offered their love and prayers.

One week, I met a beautiful new employee. I could see that she was new to the salon and somewhat nervous. "What is your name?" I asked.

In broken English she answered, "My name Tammy."

After hearing so many different names, I thought it was unique to have a name like Tammy.

Then, in a more agitated tone, she continued. "That not my name. They make me change it. My real name others have." Then Tammy proceeded to point to the other women and say, "She a Ho and she a Ho. They are many Hos that work here."

I about fell out of the pedicure chair. "Tammy," I said. "Your new name is beautiful—the best name here."

With that exchange, her anxious facial expression transformed into a sweet smile.

After a few weeks, "Tammy" understood our American slang. To this day, she and I laugh about our first meeting.

I will always have a heart connection to my lovely Vietnamese girlfriends. Even brighter than the clear topcoat on my newly polished fingernails were their caring and giving spirits. They helped me rediscover my shine.

I MET JESUS AT WALMART

I am sure Naomi looked to the heavens many times and asked, "Where are You, Lord?" Oh, yeah, haven't we all?

"I was sick," said the lovely lady to me after my presentation. "I decided to go to Walmart and walk around the store for my own sanity. I was recovering from a scary illness and had to wear a surgical mask out in public," she said. "My spirits were down since I was struggling with my faith and wondered where God was. Entering Walmart, I heard an elderly woman shout, 'Herbert, where are you?' The elderly lady was pushing her cart. Right behind her was Herbert. The somewhat hen-pecked Herbert answered in a loud voice, 'I'm right behind you, Mildred.'

"I smiled at Herbert," my friend said, "and continued on my therapeutic journey. About ten minutes later, I felt a tap on my shoulder. Surprisingly, it was Herbert.

"'Lady,' Herbert said, 'I don't know you and you don't know me but I know you are sick. I can see it in your eyes. I want to pray for you.'

"I was literally taken from behind," said my new friend. "Oh, thank you," she said to Herbert. "I appreciate your keeping me in your prayers.

"Well," continued my friend. "I thought he would pray for me during his private prayer time. Oh, was I wrong! Right there, in Walmart Supercenter, Herbert put his hands on my shoulders and began praying... loud.

"Don't get me wrong. I was very moved," she said. "But I was stuck between being touched and being tickled. And a crowd of people stood all around us. Knowing that I was standing in Walmart Supercenter between jars of pickles and bags of coffee made me laugh," she said. "My shoulders began shaking uncontrollably. And the more I shook, the louder Herbert prayed.

"'Lord, I can feel you shaking inside this lady, and you know she is sick, but she is not ready to check out!'"

After her encounter with Herbert, my friend walked to the front of the store. Feeling somewhat numb, she was ushered to the proper lane. The polite clerk asked, "Are you ready to check out?"

From behind, my friend heard, "Not according to Herbert!"

"That is when it hit me," she said. "It was the answer

to my question, 'God, where are You?' I realized that the Lord showed up at Walmart Supercenter in the form of a little old man named Herbert."

THE POWER OF HANDS

When you think about Naomi and Ruth and all they did with their hands—from nurturing their children to caring for their family to gleaning wheat—it brings to mind all that we do with our hands as women.

At my daughter's wedding, we were blessed to have our wonderful minister, Reverend Steve Keck, and Caroline's childhood minister, Paul Frey, conduct the service for Caroline and Drew's marriage ceremony. Paul's words touched our hearts and brought tears to our eyes. You will love his message delivered on October 10, 2015, at Harmony United Methodist Church in Johnston, South Carolina, on the power we have with our hands.

I want to talk about your hands...hands have been so significant in both of your lives from the moment you were born. Tender, shaking hands held both of you and held you close, and the lives of your parents were changed forever.

There was the day, Caroline, you were right here, and Wayne Horne held you in his hands. He took one of his hands and put water on your head and baptized you in the name of the Father, Son, and Holy Spirit. That day, God's hand reached out, and you became a member of this family of God as the people here promised to arrange their lives so you would know who God is and how you would come to affirm Him as your own. Hands are so important.

I can remember seeing you walk outside through the church when you were so little and hanging on to your daddy's pinky finger and running to your momma when you fell out of one of those trees over there and skinned your knee. I think I even saw you holding hands with your brother Holmes once, only once. I remember a time when we were walking over to the Grange Hall, and your momma said, "Come over here, honey, and walk with us," and you said, "I want to walk with Preacher Paul and Miss Ruth Anne." You held both of our hands as we walked across the lawn.

Caroline and I have a lot of history that goes back some twenty-two years. In fact, I've laid claim to the fact that I am the first man that Caroline ever dumped. It wasn't me alone. It was Dan Henderson and me together. We were riding out Christmas caroling. We were riding in the back of the Herlong farm truck with the hay bales around us; Holmes and Caroline were in the front seat. As we were riding down the road, Caroline said, "Daddy, what is this handle here?" Thomas said,

"*Caroline, don't touch that.*" *But Caroline was a curious child and a motivated child, so she pulled that handle, and when she did, the back of that truck started to come up, and Dan and I were in the back, and we reached across the back of that truck. Dan and I have been friends for some time, but we did not customarily hold hands, but we did that night. Trying to keep everyone from sliding off, your dad pushed that lever down. Dan said at the time it was good that we did not fall off because Jane was following behind us, and she would have run over us and then she would have backed up to see what made that bump.*

Hands have reached out to you both over the years. They have guided you, nurtured you; they have corrected you—the hands of your extended family—your grandparents, aunts, and uncles. I knew your grandparents—the strong hands of your grandfathers, the hands of both your grandmothers. Caroline, you were also named after your grandmother, Eleanor, who was known for her creative use of colorful language. Your father was afraid you might resemble her. It was you who would correct her when she used those colorful words. And I remember the words of our beloved Tootsie: "That Caroline is just like Jane ... and that be for true!"

Then the time came when you met one another, and in time, there was the day when your hands ac-

cidentally, maybe not so accidentally, brushed each other's hands. And all of a sudden, you were holding hands, and it came to be that every time you were together you were holding hands. And it just seemed so right because it is right, and here you stand together holding hands...together. Across the years and through space and time as you hold hands, it represents the hands of all those who have known you and loved you, reached out to touch you to say, "We love you, we support you, and we are here to honor and encourage you...always."

It is especially significant that we stand here in God's house as you join your hands and are married to one another in an act of worship, that you give your lives to each other as you've given your lives to Him. The one who brought you together is the one whose hand holds yours even now.

All these hands are important, yours and all the others, because life is going to bring some surprises. It will bring challenges; it may bring disappointments. It may even now and then unexpectedly pull the dump lever, and you are going to have to hang on for all you're worth, so hold hands today and always, and we will hold yours in ours.

I remember the words from Isaiah 41:13: "I am the Lord your God who holds your right hand, who says to you, 'Do not fear; I will help you through it.'" And the words from just a couple of chapters later in Isaiah 62:3: "And you will also be a crown of beauty in the hand of the Lord and a royal diadem of the hand of the Lord your God" (ESV). So hold each other, we hold you, and the Lord holds us all.

IF YOU'RE A HEALTHY WOMAN

Through all the lessons we learn and the sadness we experience, let me give you a word of warning: take care of yourself. Don't let stress overwhelm you to the point that you miss appointments with your doctors or ignore other preventative health measures. Our bodies change, and we have to be proactive and make healthy choices.

I speak at many health fairs and for many hospital groups. So many women are consumed with taking care of everyone else but themselves. I found a clever way to remind women to take care of their changing health needs. Print it out, learn it, and practice it.[39]

If You're a Healthy Woman

If you're a healthy woman, clap your hands
If you've had a mammogram, clap your hands
If your breasts you have checked, in the shower
  when you're wet
Then you're a healthy woman, clap your hands

If you've had your legs in stirrups, stomp your feet
If you've been covered with the sheet, stomp your feet

If you promise not to swear
And it's time for your Pap smear

On your legs please use some Nair
And wash your feet

Shake your bootie for the colonoscopy
Drink the fluid so the doctors they can see
If there are polyps in your tract
Have them out and be relaxed
Shake your bootie for the colonoscopy

Fan your face if you're hot all the time
And you can't sleep, till way after nine
You're afraid to sneeze
The chin hair you must tweeze
'Cause you tinkle in your drawers
WHY?
'Cause we know it's menopause!
So be a healthy woman, clap your hands!

Naomi's Flip-Flop: I think I will stay bitter and focus on me, me, me...NaoME.

Naomi's Sparkle and Shine: I will become better instead of being bitter, embrace the changes and trust God.

How can you shine in the midst of your mess-ups? With all the changes we experience as women, seek out healthy teachings and surround yourself with loving and caring people.

Chapter 8

Proverbs 31 Woman Renovated

> *Charm is deceptive, and beauty is*
> *fleeting; but a woman who fears the*
> *Lord is to be praised.*
> (Proverbs 31:30 NIV)

The woman described in Proverbs 31 is amazing. As I read this Scripture passage, I believe that she is a combination of the following: CEO, CFO, EMT, PhD, RN, psychologist, veterinarian, domestic engineer, hot momma, gourmet chef, athletic coach, shuttle driver, real estate diva, tutor, master gardener, Marine drill sergeant, pharmacist, Mother Teresa, and a splash of Oprah.

Okay, I am having massive guilt. Is this woman for real? I thought about my life as I try to achieve the Proverbs 31 Woman status and came up with a more modern version than the one provided in the King James Version of the Bible. I hope you find some humor and insight in my translation.

Verse 10: "Who can find a virtuous woman? For her price is far above rubies."

It is hard to find a good woman. Her price is above everything that sparkles and shines. If she were getting paid for being a stay-at-home mom, she would earn an annual salary of $143,102.[40]

Verse 11: "The heart of her husband doth safely trust in her, so that he shall have no need of spoil."

Her husband loves her to death, and when food spoils in the fridge, he cleans it and doesn't lecture her when green stuff forms on food because he knows she is doing 1,000 things at once.

Verse 12: "She will do him good and not evil all the days of her life."

She will be wonderful to her hubby and, like Tammy Wynette, will stand by her man. But you better not hang out too much with the guys or especially other chicks because some women like to break up marriages just 'cause they can. Bottom line—don't make Momma mad. #scornedwoman

Verse 13: "She seeketh wool, and flax, and worketh willingly with her hands."

She goes to Walmart, the mall, or shops online. Some of us don't work well with our hands, but we love manicures. Does that count?

Verse 14: "She is like the merchants' ships; she bringeth her food from afar."

Like the grocery store buggy, she transports her food or opens her shipment of meals from Simply Fresh delivered by FedEx. It does come from afar. She may think about growing a garden, or at least talk about it.

Verse 15: "She riseth also while it is yet night, and giveth meat to her household, and a portion to her maidens."

She rises in the night, is exhausted, and breastfeeds her child or helps when they throw up. She makes sure her household appliances are in working order since these are her servants.

Verse 16: "She considereth a field, and buyeth it: with the fruit of her hands she planteth a vineyard."

She may even shop around for her dream house. She has a glass of Chardonnay at times from her vineyard of various wine grapes.

Verse 17: "She girdeth her loins with strength, and strengtheneth her arms."

She has strong arms and lifts weights so if another child messes with her babies or another woman messes with her man, they are in trouble.

Verse 18: "She perceiveth that her merchandise is good: her candle goeth not out by night."

She stays up late so she can get things done without interruptions. She wears footie socks, prays no noise will wake up the family, then finally drags her weary self to bed.

Verse 19: "She layeth her hands to the spindle, and her hands hold the distaff."

She sews on buttons and fixes ripped seams or pays other people to repair clothes.

Verse 20: "She stretcheth out her hand to the poor; yea, she reacheth forth her hands to the needy."

She gets involved in breast cancer awareness groups and fund-raising for issues she is passionate about. You go, girl!

Verse 21: "She is not afraid of the snow for her

household: for all her household are clothed with scarlet."

She is not afraid of the snow but hates black ice. Sometimes she gets dramatic and acts out like our dear Scarlett O'Hara from *Gone with the Wind*. Heavens above! If some of you are not familiar with our iconic Scarlett, rent the movie.

Verse 22: "She maketh herself coverings of tapestry; her clothing is silk and purple."

She loves to dress with style and class. She knows that decent women dress for women and trashy women dress for men. She prefers cleverage (using her mind) over cleavage.

Verse 23: "Her husband is known in the gates, when he sitteth among the elders of the land."

When she walks through town, everybody knows her and her hubby. Some people think her husband is a pretty cool guy because he married her.

Verse 24: "She maketh fine linen, and selleth it; and delivereth girdles unto the merchant."

She loves to wear apparel. Her girdle is Spanx because, after having children, she needs some help keeping her fat controlled. Some of her clothes she sells at consignment shops or gives to Goodwill.

Verse 25: "Strength and honour are her clothing; and she shall rejoice in time to come."

She is strong. She knows how to handle hard times and has a great sense of humor. I am woman. Hear me snore.

Verse 26: "She openeth her mouth with wisdom; and in her tongue is the law of kindness."

She is wise since she has been there, done that. She has great girlfriends and loves to help other women with their issues. She does not gossip with the church ladies.

Verse 27: "She looketh well to the ways of her household, and eateth not the bread of idleness."

She tries her best to keep her household organized; she's busy and stays away from Little Debbie cakes (her favorite).

Verse 28: "Her children arise up, and call her blessed; her husband also, and he praiseth her."

Her children call her blessed even if she blesses them

out. As a wife and mother, she refuses to participate in "Facebook guilt," comparing her family with others. Her children and husband praise her because of her gentle reminders. "This is a good meal...y'all say something nice," or "don't I look good in this outfit?"

Verse 29: "Many daughters have done virtuously, but thou excellest them all."

She was a good daughter because her momma told her that she was, and she misses her mother every day. Sniff.

Verse 30: "Favour is deceitful, and beauty is vain: but a woman that feareth the Lord, she shall be praised."

She is confident but not conceited. She's got a lot of great things going on, but she knows they are gifts from God. She stays humble; she surrounds herself with friends who tell her the truth—in love.

Verse 31: "Give her of the fruit of her hands; and let her own works praise her in the gates."

She just walks her walks, tries her best, and doesn't have to prove a thing. She stays away from people who try to dull her shine and says to them in her sweet, Southern drawl, "Bless yo heart."

MOTHERHOOD...DID I DO GOOD?

Okay, just for fun I have written yet another parody, this time to the tune of the Beatles' song "Yesterday."[41] I call it "Motherhood."

I knew it all—I thought I understood
Now I realize I'm dumb as wood
Oh motherhood, I thought I could
Adderall
The pill I gave my son was birth control.
My hormones always are on a roll
My mouth says words I can't control
I gave birth to my brain and now I feel insane
I need therapy or a pill—where's Dr. Phil?
I feel fat
Breastfeeding made my bosoms both go flat
My husband wishes for that pouncing cat
Yesterday I could do that.

Grown and gone are they
My hair has turned gray
Don't come back to stay
You're too old to give away
Oh motherhood, it never ends I hope that I did good
I knew it all—I misunderstood
Oh motherhood, I thought I could.

Y'all visit www.janeherlong.com to hear more!

142

POTTY PRAYERS

The Proverbs 31 Woman seems to have her priorities in the right place. After all, she is known as the virtuous woman. How do we become virtuous women? I think we need to adopt a spirit of forgiveness even when it seems stupid.

Have you ever been deeply hurt by another person? The kind of hurt that you go to bed with and wake up to. We allow the hurt to follow us like a dark cloud. Yuck. Here is something I did that helped me recover from one of the worst hurts in my life. It is unorthodox, but it worked.

It is 4:00 a.m. Nature calls. As you stumble to the bathroom, your brain starts to awaken to that dark cloud of hurt. You fear that the rest of your night will be consumed with no sleep and negative thoughts. You know you are supposed to forgive and release your toxic thoughts.

Hmm. It occurs to you that at that moment of nature calling, you are, in fact, releasing toxins from your body. Why not do the same for your mind? Call it what you want, but I call it "potty prayers." Yep, flush away!

You may be thinking, *Why, Jane, that is just nasty.* Well, then change your prayers to when you wash your hair. Pour on the shampoo and sing your own version of the classic song from the musical *South Pacific*: "I'm gonna wash those toxins right out of my life and say a prayer or two..."

Or you can use the same technique to bleach away the gunk. When you are cleaning, say a few prayers for that person and scrub away the germs—same principle.

It matters not where you begin. Just get rid of poisonous thoughts and put an end to that stinkin' thinkin' that will pollute your mind. God will honor your efforts.

After sharing this suggestion as the keynote speaker at the Christian writers conference, a gentleman approached me the next day and said, "I don't like your suggestion. I spent all day on the can!"

Proverbs 31 Woman's Flip-Flop: She is too perfect.

Proverbs 31 Woman's Sparkle and Shine: She is so perfect.

How can you shine in the midst of your mess-ups? Strive to be more like this Proverbs 31 Woman but don't go on a guilt trip when you realize you are not perfect. Give yourself permission to celebrate becoming your best self.

Chapter 9

Modern-Day Women of Wisdom

Mary, the mother of Jesus, and Elizabeth had a "generational" relationship. As soon as Gabriel appeared to Mary, she went to see Elizabeth (Luke 1:39). Mary needed Elizabeth's wisdom, and Elizabeth needed Mary to bring her out of seclusion (Luke 1:24).

"The visitation," as we have come to describe Mary's trips to Elizabeth's home, contains some of the basic ingredients of any faithful home-based Christian gathering: an enthusiastic greeting by Mary (welcome), the welcome and unsurpassed joy of the host (hospitality), Elizabeth's prayerful blessing offered over another person (prayer, blessing, and intercession), and all of it bathed with the

warmth and reassurance of God's Spirit at work among God's people.[42]

Both Mary and Elizabeth needed each other. Although they were many years apart, they could share wisdom with each other for the next leg of their journeys. Both of these ladies were women of wisdom (WOW).

Where would we be without our WOW? The Bible gives us so many of these sheroes to help us learn and grow. The one big lesson they teach us is to trust God in all things. If you are wise, you will look for modern-day Elizabeths, Sarahs, Esthers, Marys, Ruths, and Naomis to live successfully when those inevitable flip-flops happen. We can also learn from those biblical ladies who made a few mistakes and totally flopped.

Here is what I see as I travel the country speaking: WOW have several things in common. They forgive others, recover from mistakes, laugh at themselves, continue learning, share with others, make sacrifices, give back, and, here is the biggie...fight insecurities. Insecurities open the door for a plethora of problems. A first cousin to being insecure is jealousy, and women can be gold medalists in this category. They look at other women and want what they have but are not willing to do what it takes to have what other women achieve. The only cure for jealousy is to develop your own gifts and stop focusing on other people. Let other gifted women motivate you to find your talents.

VIRGINIA

I met her in 1985. She became my advisor, shoulder to cry on, and unwavering friend. Virginia Dale Honeycutt moved to Edgefield County and quickly became one of my most treasured friends. She and her husband, Earl, were an amazing couple whose beautiful home told their story. Walking from room to room, guests could enjoy artwork from practically every continent. Mr. Honeycutt is credited with a number of patents for chemical processes. Although the Honeycutts lived an exciting life traveling around the world, they decided to settle in our little town.

Virginia had an amazing sense of humor. There was a brass plaque on her historic home that read *On this site in 1897, nothing happened.* I loved that plaque so much Virginia ordered one for me.

It was always special sharing Sunday worship service with her. I have seen her shoot wasps from the air with Hot Shot as we sang together in the choir. One Sunday morning a member was asked to share the children's sermon. Holding a small brown bag, he sat right by Virginia. Unbeknownst to her, the bag housed Fred, the man's pet snake. Virginia was deathly afraid of snakes. As soon as the serpent was "let out of the bag," Virginia was halfway home. Later, when we learned that Fred had passed away, Virginia sent the owner a sympathy card.

When Virginia turned ninety, she invited all her pals

and kinfolk to join her in Savannah for a weekend of fun and frivolity. She foot the bill for the entire weekend. Saturday night was the big party with food that even Paula Deen would approve of. One of Virginia's infamous nieces, who is quite the joker, leaned over and said, "Aunt Virginia, the stripper canceled, but Frank Sinatra is coming." Yes, Frank Sinatra did make an appearance and sang his heart out for Virginia. In fact, "Frank" had so much fun that he did not want to leave.

To prepare for her elder years, Virginia built a beautiful new home. She made sure there would be a place for sitters and nurses since she wanted to enjoy her later years at home. Virginia never lost her sense of humor. Tethered to an oxygen tank, Virginia made peace with her new "O$_2$" friend and transported it in a dog stroller. She affectionately referred to it as LB—"Little Bastard."

On the heels of turning ninety-two, Virginia passed away one Wednesday evening. I had visited her earlier that day. As I sat in choir rehearsal at church that night, a place filled with so many memories of Virginia, I got the call. I drove to the hospital, held her lifeless hand, and cried. She was buried in the outfit she had worn to our daughter's wedding a few weeks earlier. It was a beautiful shade of blue with a hint of sequins that sparkled and shined.

Virginia was my WOW. During the dark days of my family falling apart and my mother's illness, Virginia was my friend and mentor. She listened to what was going on in my world and let me cry. She always gave me solid advice. I absolutely loved her.

She continually thanked me for my visits, containers of soup, and fun excursions, but she was my shero. She saved me from my unhealthy thoughts and reminded me that I was blessed with a wonderful husband and children.

Virginia's family asked me to speak at her funeral. "The two things I loved about Virginia," I said at her service, "are represented in the way she said hello and good-bye. She always began her conversation with 'Well, hi there.' Virginia's words were deliberate and heartfelt. You were important to her and she let you know it. Her parting words were just as powerful. 'Well, bye now.' You see, Virginia loved people and treasured her relationships."

I concluded my tribute to Virginia by saying, "I will see her again and she will greet me saying, 'Well, hi there.' But for today, Virginia, 'Well, bye now.'"

THE WAY FORGIVENESS WORKS

Forgiving others who have wronged you does not make sense. Read that sentence again and again. So, are you giving them permission through your act of forgiveness? No, absolutely not. You are making it possible to give yourself permission to move on and are qualified to be a card-carrying WOW.

As a Christian, I have prayed through gritted teeth, saying, "I forgive them." I truly believe that a spirit of unforgiveness is flat-out dangerous since it will grip you and ruin your health. If your goal is to shine, then negative, hateful thinking will make your heart dark. You will never find that healthy shine if you continue to harbor a spirit of bitterness and resentment.

You got trouble with forgiving people? Read this next story. You will be inspired by the courage of this woman and how forgiveness changed her life.

The message of forgiveness was taken to a new level at the National Speakers Association annual convention when I heard Immaculée Ilibagiza's story. Immaculée survived the Rwandan holocaust, and through the power of her faith, she lived to tell her story. Her book *Left to Tell: Discovering God Amidst the Rwandan Holocaust* set the tone for the entire convention. Immaculée's family was brutally murdered during a killing spree that lasted three months and claimed the lives of nearly a million Rwandans.

For ninety-one days, she and seven other women huddled silently together in the cramped bathroom of a local pastor's house while hundreds of machete-wielding killers hunted for them. Holding a rosary that belonged to those who risked their lives to protect her, Immaculée spoke of the blessings that come when we choose to forgive even under the most horrendous of circumstances.[43]

My third book, *Bury Me with My Pearls*, is based on

my personal journey. In it, I use the analogy of a pearl. The book's content grew out of a chapter about forgiveness titled "The Dark Pearl." Here is an excerpt from the chapter addressing forgiveness:

> We all dread those times when a dark pearl is added to our strand of beautiful, creamy white pearls. We don't want to put that particular pearl on our priceless strand, but ironically it can become the most valuable one of all. Its value depends on how we use and display that particular pearl. It can be a treasure or a tragedy. Can you find value in this rare treasure or will you allow it to devalue your life?

What a blessing to hear Immaculée tell her story. If she can forgive those who murdered her family, why do we struggle with much less horrific circumstances?

Read *Left to Tell: Discovering God Amidst the Rwandan Holocaust*. Immaculée's story will bless you.

PENNY FROM HEAVEN

My friend, author and speaker Penny Hunt, is one of my WOW chicks. She has survived more flip-flops in her life than a mega-shoe store in Myrtle Beach. This is what makes her so special: She has been there and knows how to help other women deal with their ever-changing roles. She came to my rescue during one of the toughest times of my life. I will forever be grateful for her love and wisdom.

Here is a powerful statement from Penny's testimony that she shares in her speeches: "I found myself standing in a welfare line and only years later in a receiving line meeting the president of the United States...." Amazing, right? The following is an excerpt from her testimony, which she shares all over the country:

My growing up years were not always a happy time in our family. My parents were continually arguing, and unfortunately, during my senior year of high school, I got caught in the crossfire. By the time they drove me to Vermont and dropped me off at college, I was about as lonely as the most pathetic pup you've ever seen walking alongside the road.

Nearly ignored by my family, and with a freedom I had never known before, it didn't take long for me to find what I thought was "love" in illicit relationships. By the summer of my freshman year, I stood in front of my grandparents' fireplace, wearing a blue suit because, as my mother said, "white is for virgins," three months pregnant, crying through a civil ceremony that was supposed to be a wedding. Sadly, that marriage did not survive.

Thus began the first of my 29 moves.

Eventually, I landed a job as a GS-4 clerk/typist

and financially, at least, things began looking up. You would think I would have learned a lesson the first time around, but sadly, foolishly, I once again began looking for love in all the wrong places. My wild lifestyle went on like that for quite a while and it was not a pretty picture.

But that night, with an uncertain future and the reality of single parenthood pressing down on me, I knelt beside my bed and talked to God for the first time in a very long time.

And I believe the night I prayed, earnestly seeking God's help and then cried myself to sleep, though there were no lightning bolts or earthquakes, God heard my prayer and began to work in my life in ways I could never imagine.

My dancing school became so successful I was able to leave the typing pool and had plans underway to build my own studio. Then God surprised me. It was early fall, and I was busily answering calls and registering students. But for several days I had been receiving messages through my answering service that a Lieutenant Commander Hunt had called.

One night, he managed to reach me at home. Seeing him for the first time, and saying, "Hello," I remembered the night of crying and knew he was the man I had prayed for.

Our first date was out to dinner—with the children—and our second was to church. And that was the beginning of what is now 30 years of marriage with a man I love, who loves me back and who has not only helped me raise my children, but has given me two of his own and one of ours to love.

Not floods that separated me from my father's hospice team on the day he died in my arms with no one but my mother and I present; or the rebellion of a cherished 16-year-old runaway daughter. I thank God for her safe return and the restoration of our relationship, but for three long years I had no way of knowing if she was alive or dead.

But through it all, the glitz and glamour, the trials and tribulations God has shown me again and again that I am loved with "an everlasting love" (Jeremiah 31:3). God's precious and magnificent promises are real.[44]

Penny is a world-class devotional writer and wonderful author. You will love her inspirational book, *Bounce, Don't Break: Stories, Reflections, and Words of Encouragement Through Times of Change.*

I THINK OF LOU

With the arrival of spring and all the trimmings, I think of my grandmother Anna Louisa Walpole Jenkins, or Lou. I am named after her and proud of it.

Lou would be the textbook example of how to be

a grandmother. She wore cotton dresses complemented by pre-Sass shoes. The way her hair was rolled up and pinned almost resembled a golden crown. Lou had the look.

Her red cubed Jell-O and yellow cooked custard were delivered to your home in Mason jars any time you were sick. Lou's benne seed cookies would melt in your mouth, and her biscuits were highly anticipated at every meal.

Lou loved for us to pick her flowers. Her yard was a sea of yellow and white spring flowers. The daffodils were always a treat to find and add to the bouquet. She sat in the Charleston Green swing and gently swayed as she watched her grandchildren enjoy the gift of spring flowers. I can still hear the creaking noise of the long chains fastened to the large hooks in the ceiling. The sound was steady and soothing. Just like Lou.

What a gift to have people in your life who are like my grandmother. There is no harsh agenda, only the prayers and wishes for us to grow in love and grace. Grandmothers provide an encouraging environment so we can become all that God has in store as we continue to bloom into our spring or into another season in life.

Surrounding yourself with an environment like the one created by my grandmother is one of the best ways for all of us to have success. We need folks to speak the truth in love for our betterment, but thank God for the special role He gives to grandmothers and other nurturers. Their job is to love and encourage.

Grandmothers are God's special handiwork, created to bloom just as beautifully as the spring flowers in Lou's yard.

TOOTSIE

I am blessed to have been reared on Johns Island, South Carolina, where the mother tongue of the Sea Islands—Gullah—is the predominant language. Many people I love and respect speak this cultural dialect. This way of communicating is not restricted to one particular race; my grandfather and father, along with those born and bred on Johns Island, had command of this unique language. Sadly, every day that passes there is one less soul who understands or uses this rare, almost poetic language.

One of the most influential WOW in my life was Ruth Bligen, or "Tootsie." Her deep faith and common sense shaped my life in a myriad of ways. She taught me life lessons that stuck to me like a steaming helping of her delicious grits.

When she knew someone had hurt my feelings, she said, "Baby, I done raise you sence you was five munt old. You is a sweet chile. Don't let dat person take away the sugar Gawd done give you." Another way to express this is, do not give anyone your permission to make you feel inferior or take away your natural, God-given gifts.

Another incident involved my being corrected as a young child. "Girl, you bes learn not to do dat again. Some people never learn dey lesson. If you want to be smat, you let duh lesson be behind you. Some peoples let they lessons be in front dem." Another translation is, learn lessons the first time so you won't have to learn them over and over again.

Tootsie could read people. One time I introduced her to my new beau, who was two years older than me. She said, "Jea-un, dat boy gwine buss-up yo heart." I did not appreciate that statement one bit until her prediction came true. You better believe all future suitors required Tootsie's approval.

Tootsie was steaming mad when her light bill was mistakenly over 4,000 dollars. My mother and I drove her to the local electric co-op to fix the mistake. When Tootsie got out of the car, my mother said, "You better go with her. You know how she gets when she is really mad. She sucks her teeth." I jumped out of the car and watched the drama. Not a word was said as Tootsie slapped her bill on the counter followed by the woman on the other side of the glass door slapping the corrected bill of twenty-one dollars and fifty cents back at Tootsie. As we walked out of the building, Tootsie said, "Dey is just some peoples who dey spirit and my spirit don't like one another." Translation: There are some people you will never be able to relate to. Your spirit will offend another person's spirit and vice versa. It took me years to learn that lesson.

Tootsie was laid to rest dressed in her white usher uniform decorated with pins that represented years of service to her beloved church. Looking at her peaceful face, I smiled, knowing Tootsie was hearing the words spoken by the Master in Matthew 25:21 that she had lived to hear: "Well done, my good and faithful servant" or, to quote the Gullah Bible: "E bossman ansa say, 'Ya done good. Ya a good wokman wa true ta e bossman! 'Cause A able fa trus ya fa do a leetle job, now A gwine gii ya chaage oba plenty big ting. Come hab a good time long wid ya bossman!' "[45]

WOW IN TEXAS

I had the honor of speaking to the Abilene Woman's Club in Abilene, Texas. Like I told one of my friends, "This group of women don't do small." I could go on and on about the wonderful rock-star treatment I received and the privilege of speaking at the beautiful, historic Paramount Theatre, but that is not what made the event special. The women of the Abilene Woman's Club care about their community and are passionate about helping others.

From the first phone call, Abilene Club member Debbie Blake shared her vision for this fund-raising event. I knew my visit would be extraordinary. When I met Debbie, I was so impressed with her exceptional desire to serve her community. She mentioned one volunteer event and fund-raiser after another. Remarkably, Debbie has lived in Abilene for only eight years. Even at Halloween, Debbie hosted over 2,800 trick-or-treaters. What a servant's heart!

When I arrived at the Abilene Woman's Club for a reception and book signing, I met another remarkable servant, Dr. Virginia Connally. At the age of 101, this Energizer Bunny is still going strong. Dr. Connally is a retired ENT and has committed her life to helping others. An avid reader, Dr. Connally told me about the latest book she had read, *Rich Christians in an Age of Hunger*, written by Ronald J. Sider. Dr. Connally said, "We have to do more to help others." She walks her talk. After my speech the next evening, Dr. Connally introduced me to her missionary friends who were visiting with her. How does Dr. Connally stay so active? Maybe you should ask her personal trainer, who works out with her three times a week.

I read an article about Dr. Connally in *Baptist Today*: "Dr. Connally is a gracious person with a quick mind and wit. She attracts people like bugs to a light—whether a down-and-out stranger or those in positions of power."[46]

The wonderful radio personality Terry Diamond was another star who sparkled like a ten-carat diamond when I met her. Terry did everything in her power to make this event a ringer.

So if you want to feel better and have the go-getter attitude, visit the Abilene Woman's Club and chat with some of the biggest and brightest stars in the Lone Star State. Their lesson is that you can change your world when you give unconditionally of yourself, regardless of your age.

Women of wisdom are volunteers and philanthropists. They have a heart for service. If you want to shine with confidence, get involved and give back.

A ROCK AND A CLOWN NOSE

I have come to the realization that a rock and a clown nose represent principles of successful living. I discovered this life lesson at the funeral of my dear friend Eileen Klein.

As Eileen lay in her hospital bed, nearing death's door, she asked me to sing at her funeral. The song she chose was "We'll Meet Again." Eileen and I had a most unusual relationship of strange humor, so I replied, "Yes, Eileen. I will be honored to sing at your funeral, but I am singing a song I just wrote titled, 'She Lost Her Virginity at the Waffle House.'" We both had a good laugh.

I was out of town when I received the call that Eileen had passed away. I was thankful her suffering was over. My problem was that the airline (whose name I will not mention but it rhymes with the word *skelta*) canceled my flight that evening and rebooked me on the 1:40 p.m. flight the next afternoon. Eileen's funeral was scheduled for 11:00 a.m. I speak on the topic of having a good attitude when things go wrong, so once again, I had to live the message or I needed to stay home. "Okay, Lord," I whispered, "showtime for you."

Soon an "angel" appeared and handed me his $800 ticket with an 8:30 a.m. departure time. The young man had heard me say that I promised my friend that I would sing at her funeral. I arrived at the funeral at 10:30 a.m.

During the service, the priest honored Eileen in a lovely way. He mentioned her fabulous sense of humor. Her daughter, Kerry, spoke of her mother with passion and conviction. She mentioned that her mother had a box full of clown noses and that she enjoyed collecting rocks. Kerry told the congregation that she wanted all of us to have one of Eileen's rocks.

I was supposed to sing my song right before the benediction, but the priest completely forgot to introduce me. I thought of that box filled with clown noses and Eileen's rock collection and, in a strange way, it gave me courage. I jumped from my seat knowing I had promised to sing. And with all the trouble I had overcome to get to the funeral, by the grace of God, it was going to happen. I stood at the podium and sang my heart out for my dear friend Eileen.

Yes, Eileen, you are so right. What we all need in this life is a clown nose to remind us of the importance of having a good sense of humor, and a rock—something firm to lean on in times of trouble.

We will meet again, my friend.

SHE RODE THE COW

"Miss Sally empowered us." Those words were spoken by my dear friend Leize Willis. Leize called, and in between sobs told me that our wonderful mentor and straight-shooting friend, Miss Sally, had passed away. She helped both Leize and me through the dark times and gave us the courage to do the next right thing.

A friend of mine said, "I have watched Miss Sally face terrible challenges, and she faced them with incredible courage, faith, and amazing grace." Miss Sally Hanckel was my earthly cheerleader who helped me develop courage, faith, and grace. I just loved her.

A client friend of mine sent me a magnet for my fridge. We have a mutual love of exchanging quotes. Our last magnet exchange cited words from Helen Keller: "Life is a daring adventure or nothing."

I really like that one. I feel like I am a daring person, but there are those who cross my path who totally amaze me. Miss Sally Hanckel was one brave, daring woman. Without going into a pile of details, believe me... she was brave. First of all, Miss Sally had six children. That is an adventure in itself.

Every time I buy Coburg milk, I think of Miss Sally since the Hanckels owned the dairy. Anyone who has a dairy business or has visited Charleston enough is probably familiar with Coburg Dairy. The monument to Coburg still stands or spins on Highway 17. It is the infamous cow. At Christmas, the traditional cow is replaced with a red and green one along with a carton of Coburg eggnog. Sometimes the cow is more chocolate-colored accompanied with, of course, a carton of chocolate milk. Being that it spins, you know, you just want to ride the thing.

I got to know Miss Sally at Sunday brunch after early church at St. Johns Island Café on Johns Island. That quaint restaurant was filled with Episcopalians and sprinkled with a few token Yankees. (We really like these Yankees because they don't like Yankees either.) I mustered the courage to ask Miss Sally if she ever rode the cow. I just knew the answer would be yes. I was close! She said, "I made it to the platform but never to the top of the cow." Still, that is admirable.

The cow was one landmark in Charleston that attracted the young or young at heart. The other was Shoney's Big Boy. Big Boy looked like a huge Elvis dressed in checkered "hogwashers," holding up a hamburger. All of us wanted to sit on that hamburger. We talked about it so much that we finally gave it a try. Well, sitting on the cow had to be next. Just as we had made our plans to ride the cow, Coburg put up a barbed-wire fence to keep us out. Oh well, so much for the cow ride.

Sitting on the hamburger was easy; the cow was tough. If you made it to the cow, everybody knew about it. You became kind of a celebrity. Sitting on the hamburger was just so-so.

The question is, are you going to sit on the hamburger or ride the cow? Although I never made it to the cow, I still want to ride that thing.

I hope we all want to try and do different things in our lives. Take a risk and do something out of the norm. For lack of a better way to say it, ride the cow. Helen Keller was right: "Life is a daring adventure or nothing."

Thank you, Miss Sally, for teaching me and many others how to live with courage and faith, for showing us how to make life one daring adventure.

MY SISTAH, ANNA

I have a real biblical Anna in my life and, ironically, her name is also Anna. Biblical Anna is known as the woman who became the first Christian missionary (Luke 2:36–38).[47] She was a prophetess and prayer warrior, and never hesitated to share her faith with others. All these wonderful qualities describe my modern-day WOW, Anna.

When my mother was a child, she was awakened by the sound of garden rakes and hoes hitting the packed soil. Outside the window, Momma saw the hardworking children of the Fields family weed the crop. At 5:00 a.m., this farm family was doing chores before school, and they repeated those tasks after school. My parents had great respect for this family of African Americans.

Through the years, I watched Daddy and Robbie

Fields help each other as they prepared the land and gathered crops during the Johns Island growing season. They had a wonderful relationship built on mutual respect.

One of the things I loved about the Fields family was the fun relationship they had with my mother. Momma started an interesting competition with Robbie and his U-pick stand. She figured out how to make money after Daddy finished harvesting his tomato crop. The only problem was Fields U-Pick was listed in the *Post and Courier* alphabetically before Jenkins U-Pick, so Momma decided to change her U-pick name to A1 U-Pick. Can you believe that?

After Daddy passed away, my mother continued to live down the dirt road on the farm all by herself. As my mother's health declined, I was more and more concerned about her living alone. She would not move closer to me, so I made the three-hour trip to Johns Island several times a month. I was very concerned about her health, safety, and spiritual life.

One day, sweet Anna called Momma and asked if she could live with her while her new home was being built. This was an answer to my prayer.

Momma loved every minute with Anna. They laughed together, cried together, and prayed together. Anna made Jesus Christ real to my mother. Just like biblical Anna, she shared her faith with my mother. If I had any doubts about Momma's eternal home, Anna, my modern-day prayer warrior and missionary, made sure my mother's bags were packed for her new heavenly home. I love this woman.

It grieves me to see so many racial issues in our country, but I am thankful to know a different world. I am blessed that my father and mother loved and cared for the wonderful men and women who worked on our family farm. I saw my father cry when one of his workers was diagnosed with diabetes. Many trips were made to the doctor as my mother transported and paid for medical expenses for so many who needed care. When my daddy died, I heard countless stories of his many acts of kindness. A migrant worker who worked on the farm planted a rosebush on Daddy's grave and credits him for her desire to become a certified public accountant.

I share this backstory to say these wonderful people are my family. They know that my parents were good people, kind and generous. These folks are so good to me, and I feel their genuine love. Anna is my sistah. The Lord answered my prayers with this prayer warrior.

After Momma made her trip to heaven, Anna continued to live at the house until her new home was built. She was there when my mother's health flip-flopped and helped my mother with other family heartaches. What a blessing she was and continues to be in my life. I know my mother is sparkling in her heavenly attire while I continue to shine on earth because of the woman I affectionately refer to as my sistah, my modern-day Anna.

THE YELLOW TRAY

It was the time in my life that I dreaded: life without my mother. My mother passed away peacefully at Roper Hospital in Charleston, South Carolina, on July 7, 2009. That date was celebrated years ago as the anniversary of my winning the title of Miss South Carolina, which led to my competing for the title of Miss America. Now that date has a whole new meaning. I was beside her, holding her hand, as she drew her last breath.

I knew the days and weeks ahead would be met with many tears and emotional moments. Thank the Lord for the WOW who called, prayed with me, and shared wonderful meals.

One afternoon, I heard a car door slam and the friendly greeting of my friend Suzie. Suzie is a fantastic cook, and her bright smile and cheery demeanor were a welcome sight.

"I brought you supper," said Suzie with a hug and a smile. She had transported the dishes on an old, yellow lunchroom-style tray. "Oh, just throw that tray in the trash. I think I stole it from the school lunchroom," Suzie said, then laughed.

The yellow tray stayed on my counter for days. For some reason, I could not get rid of it. It reminded me of an infamous yellow pan from my childhood. When we heard my mother say, "Hurry, get the yellow pan!" someone was either sick or had another type of emergency. That yellow pan was our remedy to meet a need. For some reason, I felt the same way about the yellow tray. It was special.

Only a few weeks later, I got the news that one of our wonderful church members had lost their son. Many were heartbroken for this family since they were pillars in our church and community. We all wanted to share our love and condolences with them. I thought about the yellow tray; I knew what to do.

I realized that tray had a purpose. It was not trash; it was a treasure. I loaded it with my best dishes, drove to the family's home, and presented it to my friend. That tray became known as the yellow tray of friendship. I told my friend the story and suggested that we pass it on to the next family who has a loss. The tray's message: prepare your best dishes and pass it on.

And you know who got the tray next? I did. Only five months after losing my mother, my sister died. My friend came to my house with her best dishes loaded on that yellow tray. The only difference was that her granddaughter had decorated the tray with large purple letters that read, *The Yellow Tray of Friendship*.

This is what WOW are all about. They cry with us, pray for us, and intuitively know we need a lunch date, a girlfriend trip, or a day of shopping. To receive this kind of love and nurturing from WOW, you must become a WOW. What a special blessing to help other women through their issues and trying times.

Give your best. It may be represented in a symbol

like a yellow tray, a certain culinary skill you have perfected, or a physical gift. I am referring to something
that is unique to you. Giving your best reminds me
of the doxology said after the offering, from the 1928
Book of Common Prayer: "All things come of thee, O
Lord, and of thine own have we given thee..."[48]

BEAUTY QUEEN BOTTOMS UP

WOWs take care of their health and pay special attention to hormonal changes that become more aggressive
at the age of forty. Even former beauty queens admit to
priorities changing from winning a pageant to wearing
the crown of good health.

It happens every five years. The Miss South Carolina
Pageant hosts an anniversary of former title holders.
The most fun experience is usually the luncheon held
during pageant week. We all get together, share memories, and discuss what we are doing.

I am so proud of my Miss SC sistahs! They are
Nashville radio personalities, authors, professional
singers, Broadway stars, and Hollywood actresses.
Some have chosen to focus on their amazing children.
One of our former Miss South Carolinas is Nancy
Humphries. You may know her as Nancy O'Dell, star
of *Entertainment Tonight*.

At one of our luncheons, several of our Miss SCs
were sharing about their new book or newly released

recordings, plus other accomplishments. The eldest of the Miss South Carolinas was the last to speak. As beautiful as ever, she stood up to share her latest accomplishment. I will never forget what she said: "Well, I have you all beat. I just had a perfect colonoscopy."

It was a moment that put life in its proper perspective. No matter how accomplished you may be, good health is one of the most important gifts you can give yourself. This was her moment for a different kind of sparkle and shine!

CANDI MISSED ONLY ONE MAMMOGRAM

I have chosen to take somewhat of a detour to share this story about my dear, funny college roommate, Candi. With so much needed attention on the fight against the cruel disease cancer, I am sharing this story to encourage all women to never skip a mammogram. WOW take care of their health. I hope this next story will be a reminder of how important it is to never neglect your health.

A few years ago, I spent a week in Minnesota to speak for an electric co-op and to visit my Columbia College roommate who was battling stage 4 breast cancer.

After my speech in Red Wing, Minnesota, I headed back to the big city of Minneapolis to see Candi. It is one of those decisions you make to go and just be there. I had no idea what I would encounter as I drove into her mother's driveway where Candi was staying for her final round of radiation therapy at the Mayo Clinic. She had been recently informed that there was nothing else the doctors could do for her.

Candi was standing in her mother's den looking much different from the way she had looked when I had seen her the year before. The chemotherapy had robbed her of her beautiful hair, and there was a scar down the side of her head where surgery had been performed. Her left arm hung lifeless at her side, but her beautiful eyes were still sparkling and her smile was radiant.

We packed her things and off we went to her home after a two-week stay with her mother. We had dinner at her favorite restaurant, where we received much attention from waiters and waitresses who love her dearly. Candi was delighted when we arrived at her home. I helped her make up her bed with the new jungle-print sheets she had ordered. Her spirits lifted and her personality began to shine once again.

The next day we had another enjoyable meal at the Good Earth Restaurant. We then drove to the Mayo Clinic—a four-hour round-trip for a fifteen-minute treatment. While Candi was having her radiation treatment, I was instructed to wait at a gift shop across the street. The shop owner had met Candi only once, but in typical Candi style, she'd made another lifelong friend. We had dinner with many of Candi's new "Mayo angels," laughing and reminiscing.

Our time together was a mental vacation from the

obviously long battle and the many prayers that a new treatment involving Eastern medicine will conquer this evil disease that had changed her life forever.

Candi and I made plans to rendezvous in Charleston the following September. As my mother always said, "Where there is life, there is hope."

As I drove away from her lovely home, I had a strange feeling that I would not see Candi again on this side of heaven. My beautiful, funny roomie, who lived with so much passion and love in her heart, died two months later.

Candi is a WOW because despite illness she continued to have hope, give to others, and maintain a positive attitude. Rarely did I see her in a pitiful state.

Candi also loved and cared for her amazing mother, Micki. After Candi passed away, I called her mother. I was so concerned that Micki would be in a pit of grief. I was wrong. Micki told me that Candi was a blessing in her life and she was focusing on the wonderful moments they shared.

Hearing how Micki had chosen to handle the loss of her daughter was another WOW moment. Her grief was genuine, but Micki refused to be consumed with a spirit of grief.

Candi missed only one mammogram and paid a heavy price. There are many other women who have never missed a mammogram and suffered the same diagnosis. Just remember, take care of your mind and body.

WOW SHEROES

We cannot put a price on our WOW friends who come to our rescue during difficult times. Kim Becking is one of these sheroes. She has discovered a unique way to help other women dealing with breast cancer. Kim wrote a clever book titled *Nordie's at Noon*.

This book is a true story about Kim and her three friends who gathered monthly to support each other as they bravely battled breast cancer. The following is Kim's description of *Nordie's at Noon*:

The book shares personal stories of four young professional women diagnosed with breast cancer at the age of 30 or younger. Once a month, they met at Café Nordstrom for lunch and a little retail therapy. It was their special place to laugh, cry, and celebrate the journey of life after a cancer diagnosis.

Their breast cancer diagnoses came at very different phases of their young lives. Patti was 24, single, and forging her way in the corporate world. Jana was planning her wedding at age 27, and bravely walked down the aisle wearing a wig and breast prosthesis. Jennifer, also 27, was five months pregnant when she was diagnosed, and endured surgery and chemotherapy during the pregnancy. Kim found her lump at age 30 while planning her son's second birthday party, and faced the issues of raising a toddler while she underwent treatment.[49]

Nordie's at Noon is a source of humor, strength, inspiration, and education. Kim's hope is that this book will encourage women to be proactive with their health and to realize that no one is "too young" for breast cancer.

Never pass up a chance to be a WOW for others.

SIXTEEN WOW LESSONS

People often tell Regina Brett how great she looks for her age. Turns out, she is actually fifty-four years old—not ninety. She wrote down these life lessons the night before her forty-fifth birthday after being diagnosed with breast cancer. Over the past decade, these lessons have gone viral on the Internet amid claims that she is ninety years old. Luckily, she finds humor in this misrepresentation, knowing how many lives she has touched.

Regina wrote forty-five of these lessons; I have highlighted my top sixteen and added a few personal comments.[50] Whatever your age might be, these universal lessons are relatable to anyone who needs a reminder of what's important in life.

1. When in doubt, take the next small step.

I was not chosen to be in the Little Miss Merry Christmas Pageant, but they used my fishbowl for the contestants to retrieve questions. I did not have the "stick-out" dress or poodle socks, but I did have the fishbowl. Basically, you gotta start somewhere. A dream was born in my soul that evening as I watched the older high school girls with their beehive updos, chiffon gowns, and long white gloves reach into my fishbowl. Eighteen years and five months later, I walked across the stage of the Miss America Pageant.

2. Life is too short to waste time hating anyone.

Hate is a good way to ruin your life.

3. You don't have to win every argument. Agree to disagree.

This is one of the best secrets for alleviating stress. Pick your battles wisely and do not major in the minors.

4. Make peace with your past so it won't screw up the present.

I say learn from your past. There are two types of people to study from—winners and losers. Also, forgive yourself and others.

5. Don't compare your life to others. You have no idea what their journey is all about.

Don't pretend you are an expert in other people's issues. It is an insult to them and makes you look foolish.

6. If a relationship has to be a secret, you shouldn't be in it.

7. Life is too short for long pity parties. Get busy living, or get busy dying.

8. It's never too late to have a happy childhood. But the second one is up to you and no one else.

I love this quote. It gets on my nerves when people blame their behavior on their childhood, genes, and so on. There are wonderful counselors who can help you sift through buried issues once and for all. Do yourself a favor and get fixed.

9. When it comes to going after what you love in life, don't take no for an answer.

I live by this quote. I say, prove them wrong.

10. The most important sex organ is the brain.

Yep, my passion lies between my eyes.

11. Frame every so-called disaster with these words: "In five years, will this matter?"

I need to be reminded of this lesson. Other questions to ask yourself are "Is it possible?" and "Is it probable?"

12. What other people think of you is none of your business.

Nice! I just had to repeat this rhinestone of wisdom. In this case, being ignorant about idle talk may be a gift you give to yourself.

13. Your children get only one childhood. Make it memorable.

14. If we all threw our problems in a pile and saw everyone else's, we'd grab ours back.

15. Envy is a waste of time. You already have all you need.

Here is how I handle envy. When that nasty monster shows up, I decide to get to know the person. It is amazing what you discover. Another great quote about envy is from Zig Ziglar: "You will get all you want in life if you help enough other people get what they want."[51] Even if they want what you want. It works.

16. No matter how you feel, get up, dress up, and show up.

To quote Zig again, "No matter how you feel, get up, dress up, show up, and never give up!"[52] Also, watch how people treat you when you dress up.

WOW 'EM WITH HUMOR

"A person without a sense of humor is like a wagon without springs—jolted by every pebble in the road."

Henry Ward Beecher

The older I become, the more I love to find the humor in life. Here are a few funnies that will make you LOL or at least snicker.

I was speaking in Winchester, Virginia, around Valentine's Day, and I mentioned to the audience that it warms a wife's heart to be given fancy lingerie. After the program, a sweet young woman approached me and said how glad she was I had made that suggestion. "My husband only buys me them Hanes Her Way drawers that come up real high. They is nice drawers and got the cotton crotch, but I sure would like some of them fancy high-cut drawers. The only thing I got in my house that is French cut is my green beans."

* * *

One of my first appearances in Edgefield County was singing at the local nursing home. I recorded some big band music and loved singing for the residents. At the conclusion, one dear sainted senior gingerly stood, clapping. "Honey, did you see what I did?" asked the sweet resident.

"Oh, yes, ma'am!" I replied.

"Well," she continued, "you don't know how tough it is at my age to give anyone a standing *ovulation*."

I commented to another resident how pretty she looked.

"How could I?" the resident exclaimed. "Three times I have had my heart *castrated*."

* * *

My elderly aunt decided to tackle the drive-thru at McDonald's. It was her first try and she was rather nervous. She stopped her car, rolled down her window, and leaned into what she thought was the speaker to place her order. "I'll have a cheeseburger," she announced in a loud voice. She heard nothing. Once again, with a stronger voice, she said, "Hello, I'll have a cheeseburger, please." Still nothing. She glanced in her rearview mirror and realized that she had a string of cars behind her. It was her third and final attempt. Just as she leaned closer in to place her order, a gentleman from the car behind her made his way to her car door. "Lady," he said politely, "you are talking to a trash can."

* * *

As I was signing books one time, a woman told me her name was "Walk-a-line." Then she proceeded to tell me how she got her name. On the way to the hospital to be born, her father was pulled over for reckless driving. The officer thought her father was drunk and gave him a sobriety test. Bless her heart, they did not make it to the hospital on time. She was born in the backseat of that car. To celebrate her birth, she was appropriately named "Walk-a-line."

* * *

Not long ago, I called my teacher friend and asked her if anything funny had happened to her recently. She told me that when she had substituted one day, she announced to the children that she was their "substitute" teacher. Later on, one of the kindergarten students announced to another teacher that they had a "prostitute" teacher that day.

* * *

Another friend of mine teaches children of inmates. These are precious little ones, but they have seen and heard so much at a young age. My friend told the class that she had found a large snake wrapped around the leg of her kitchen table that morning.

One little boy asked, "What did you do?"

She said, "I ran next door to get the hoe."

Then he exclaimed, "What did she do?"

OUR BEST CONCEALED WEAPON—HUMOR

Penny and I decided to obtain our CWP (concealed weapons permit). We both attended class, and Penny, the great note taker, wrote down every word. We were given specific instructions on what to do if stopped by a police officer. Penny attends to detail like no one I have ever seen.

About a month after receiving our CWP, Penny called. "Jane, I got pulled over in Bamberg for speeding. I did everything our instructor said to do when you get pulled over. I wrote it down word for word. I kept my hands on the steering wheel till my knuckles turned white. I did not move since the officer knew I had a concealed weapon. You know, they cross-check your license.

"Jane, it was awful!" Penny lamented. "He just kept knocking on my window, yelling, 'Lady, roll down your window!' I just could not believe how insistent he was. He was practically beating on my window! Finally, I said, 'Officer, I cannot move to roll down my window. I have a concealed weapon!'

"'Yes, ma'am,'" replied the officer. "'Where is it?'"

Looking straight ahead, with white-knuckled hands, Penny replied, "At home."

SHOULDA...WOULDA...COULDA

For some reason, I have been hearing the words *shoulda, woulda, coulda*. If you want to live as a WOW, avoid these words. I am paying extra attention to them since I am older and hopefully wiser. I thought it would be interesting to dissect the meaning.

Woulda and *coulda*. I think these are excuse words. Here is an example: "I woulda/coulda but_____ _____." Another way to say the same thing with personal accountability is, "I could have done more."

Shoulda. This word has been officially added to my list of things never to say. I have a plaque in my house that reads, *Destined to be an old woman with no regrets. Shoulda* is a regret word. I have heard unhappy people use this word often. They can't fix "it" or try something different because it is too late.

To avoid the shoulda moments, look ahead. Ask yourself what life will look like in twenty years. If you see yourself unhappy and full of regrets, change your course.

My mother said something years ago that made me laugh. I told her that some individuals are encouraged to write a letter to deceased people who still "haunt" them with unresolved issues or regrets. Her response was typical "all Eleanor." She paused, looked at me, tilted her head, and said, "How do you address the letter—GRAVE?"

This suggestion made no sense to her, which explains why she lived to be in her eighties and died peacefully. I witnessed how she handled a heartbreaking event with love, grace, and forgiveness.

So watch out for the woulda, shoulda, coulda moments in life. Strive to have no regrets and live with greater self-respect.

I HIT THE BOTTLE

In honor of the aging process, I wrote a song. The lyrics put into perspective the value of time as we grow in becoming WOW, the women God designed us to be. (Words by Jane Jenkins Herlong; music by Jane Jenkins Herlong and Mike Smith)

> *I looked in the mirror and what did I see?*
> *A gray-haired women looking at me*
> *Fine lines and wrinkles, gone was her twinkle*
> *Fearin' a sneeze might make her tinkle*
> *So I hit the bottle*
>
> *Give me a swig of Mary Kay*
> *I'll lick a jar of Oil of Olay*
> *Lady Clairol and Maybelline*
> *Take me back to when I was sixteen*
> *Do I want to be sixteen again?*

I looked in the mirror and what did I see?
Bad skin and braces lookin' at me
Hair so frizzy filled with split ends
Desperately searchin' for a boyfriend
So I hit the bottle

Clearasil, a splash of Sea Breeze
Dippity-do and Aussie Freeze
Drink up the O.J.
Be healthy and fair
But I need those cans to roll my hair
I thought of the many trials I'd been through
Time has passed; now I know what to do
So I looked in the mirror and what did I see?
A gray-haired woman, as wise as can be.
So let's celebrate and not complain
Give me a bottle of champagne!

BE A WOW TO YOURSELF

If you take to heart many of the lessons our biblical ladies teach about dealing with flip-flops and you surround yourself with modern-day WOW, you may be surprised by your reaction when the next mess-up pops up. We all know that stuff happens, but how we handle stuff is what reveals the heart of our character. Here is what happened to me.

I had just been accused of a lie that cut my heart. I was

stunned but also amazed at how calm I was as I heard a litany of lies and accusations. I was listening to verbiage that was a clear example of unhealthy anger that had gripped someone's character. Years ago, this same person would never have done or thought to do such a thing. I was witnessing a heartbreaking personality flip-flop.

Anger can be a dangerous emotion. The Bible warns us about how to handle anger wisely without letting it control you. Ephesians 4:26 says, "Be angry but do not sin" (RSV). A counselor told me that sustained anger can manifest itself in mental illness.

After that cell phone conversation ended, I walked into my home totally shocked. My sweet Caroline was watching the movie *Batman Returns*.

"Momma, sit with me and watch this movie," said Caroline, not knowing what had just happened.

After a few moments, the dialogue between Catwoman and her evil accomplice, the Penguin, caught my attention. Catwoman said, "To destroy Batman, we must first turn him into what he hates the most. Namely us."[53]

I am telling you, it was a divine moment of truth. The message was clear: if you retaliate with the same kind of behavior, you are no better than the person attacking you.

Really, Jane? So God spoke to you through Catwoman? Yes, He did. In Numbers 22:28 He spoke through a donkey: "Then the Lord gave the donkey the ability to speak" (NLT). So, if the Lord can speak through a donkey, He can certainly communicate through Catwoman.

After the truth was known and the issued handled, it was suggested that I retaliate since a false report was filed. I chose not to. I have learned that the best way to destroy your life is to harbor anger and bitterness in your heart. Instead, I approached this person, asked to see the damage, and offered to pay for what I was accused of doing. Instead, that person shamefully hung her head.

Here is the point—I was surprised at how I responded; I wowed myself. I believe the only way to be a WOW is to read, pray, listen to, and study the Word of God and other books to help you deal with moments that can flip you out.

I challenge you to be prepared for life's flip-flops by becoming a WOW. It will be one of the greatest gifts you give yourself. The eyes of other women will be on you. They will watch how you handle yourself, and if you can be a WOW, they will come to you for help.

Dare I say that, like Batman, you may also become someone else's hero?

Chapter 10

Mary, Did You Know?

*"I am the Lord's servant," Mary
answered. "May your word to me be
fulfilled."*

(Luke 1:38 NIV)

M ary, Did You Know?" is my favorite song to
sing at Christmas. I recorded this song on a
Christmas CD and had to perform it several
times in the recording studio without my voice cracking
with emotion. If you pay close attention to the words, it
is a tough song to sing. Anyone who has been a parent
or has parented a child can feel Mary's awe in being the
mother of the Son of God.

I asked Thomas who his favorite biblical woman
was. He said, "Mary, the mother of Jesus. She was
obedient and had a heart filled with the purest form
of humor—joy." Luke 1:46–55 records Mary's song.
Here's part of it:

And Mary said:
"My soul glorifies the Lord
and my spirit rejoices in God my Savior,
for he has been mindful
of the humble state of his servant.
From now on all generations will call me blessed,
for the Mighty One has done great things for me—
holy is his name."

Mary was filled with joy but there was a major flip-flop for "betrayed" hubby, Joseph.

If pregnancy occurred before the wedding, this was not a problem because the parentage of the child was secured. What is shocking is that Mary is pregnant and Joseph knows he is not the father. The problem is not that a betrothed couple had sex, but that presumably Mary had sex with another man—she committed adultery.[54]

This explains Joseph's reaction to divorce her, for that was the legal remedy when faced with infidelity during the betrothal period. And as Matthew tells us, Joseph wanted a quiet, "no fault" divorce (Matthew. 1:19).[55]

Coupled with great honor is sacrifice. What is Mary's first sacrifice? She lost her reputation. There are other biblical women who have had major moral flip-flops, but God, in His wisdom, placed these women in the lineage of Jesus.

Finally, some argue that Matthew is emphasizing

Mary's marginality by highlighting four immoral women in Jesus' genealogy: Tamar, Rahab, Ruth, Bathsheba (called the wife of Uriah the Hittite; see Matthew. 1:2–17). However, it is arguable that all four have histories of faithfulness in the face of troubles. Tamar is credited with doing the right thing in holding her father-in-law accountable for failing to look after her. Ruth is repeatedly praised for her obedience to her mother-in-law and to Boaz. Bathsheba was taken from her home by King David, and the text places no blame on her for his misdeed. Only Rahab is identified as a prostitute, but in saving the Hebrew spies and siding with Israel, she redeemed herself and her family—she is a heroine of the story.[56]

Have you ever known in your heart that you were doing the right thing, even though you were terribly criticized? We will never fully understand what Mary, the mother of Jesus, went through, but we have our own "villages and synagogues" to deal with. And there are the church ladies who love to shoot their wounded. I wonder how many of these busy ladies gossiped about Mary? Bless their hearts and God love 'em.

Mary also had to watch her son suffer on the cross for a crime he did not commit. I thought of Jesus many times as I dealt with a family problem that never seemed to end.

Taking a stand to honor my father's wishes for my mother as the surviving spouse was one of the most difficult times of my life. I cried and pleaded with God to "remove this cup" from me. It was an impossible mess, but God chose to allow me to go through it and not around it. My reputation was ruined in the eyes of many I cared about, but in the process, I grew in wisdom. I heard gossip and was accused of awful things. For whatever reason, those I loved did not care enough to seek the facts and truth; they chose to believe whatever worked for them. We all have to accept the fact that the seemingly distorted thoughts of others are their reality, and there is nothing we can do about it. Thomas so wisely says, "Everyone has the right to their opinions, but no one has the right to distort the facts."

Years after my mother's passing and the heartbreak of my sister's untimely death, I can see God's purpose. I learned many lessons that I share in my books and speeches. I understand that there are many people in your life who know what is going on but will not get involved to help. One of the most important acts of faith is to let God fight your battles—He will win every time.

Don't expect a superhero to fly in and right the wrongs. I have learned that through stressful times and unbearable pressure, God will show you other people's hearts. I learned the power of forgiveness when it makes no sense to forgive. The most important lesson is that, like so many biblical women, we need to turn to God for help. Get on your knees praying and off the phone talking. My friends are going to LOL at that one!

SING YOUR SONG

When I was a teenager, I heard a song that nailed my thoughts and future goals. It was a song Barbra Streisand sang, titled "Don't Rain on My Parade" from the musical *Funny Girl*.

Maybe the song captured my attention since the lyrics were motivational. Maybe it spoke to me because it was about rain. Being a farmer's daughter, I know that rain can be a blessing and a curse. When I heard that song, it was fuel to my soul. The lyrics addressed so many issues that I was struggling with. We lived in a tenant house that Daddy renovated. I was told that I had a low IQ, I was dyslexic, and I was not college material. Daddy did not have the money to pay for college. Time and time again, I heard the words *no*, *can't*, and *never*.

I would listen to that song, pray, and promise myself that I would break through those barriers. I would prove the skeptics and naysayers wrong. And I did. I entered a small Methodist college on academic probation paid for by a grant and cucumber rebate money from Daddy's failed cucumber crop. When I graduated from college, I was on the Dean's List for academic achievement. I then went to graduate school. I won the title of Miss South Carolina and that pageant's talent award; I competed in the Miss America Pageant. The pageant staff named me Miss Congeniality, and I walked the Miss America runway. I became a professional speaker and singer, have performed at Radio City Music Hall, and spoken in front of an audience of 20,000 people on live television. I became an Amazon bestselling author and my comedy is featured on SiriusXM Radio. In the summer of 2016, I was inducted into the Speaker Hall of Fame and named an *Elysian* magazine's Woman of Distinction. I do not say all of these things to brag. I am bragging on what the Lord has done in my life. I never gave up and neither should you.

Do you have a song or a system in place to keep you motivated? Something that makes you excited to get you up in the morning? Something that helps you fight all the negative influences that try to pollute your life and contaminate your future?

As a professional singer, I like to close my presentations many times with the song "Don't Rain on My Parade." Find your song, meditate on it, and listen to it—especially when those inevitable flip-flops come your way.

WONDER WOMEN

This book began with a story of my first encounter with womanhood. Then there was Deceived Eve, the first mother in the Bible. I ended with Mary, the mother of Jesus. I have always been impressed with stories of certain women of the Bible. The women I have written about are major characters, and they changed history.

This should resonate with all women since both Eve and Mary dealt with major flip-flops. They both suffered and they are both celebrated. Women have so much influence. It is up to every one of us to accept the fact that life is full of events that challenge our faith. Stuff happens, ladies.

Like Eve, find your paradise; unlike Eve, have the wisdom to be thankful and satisfied. Always strive to be more, but be cautious about wanting it all since it may cost you all.

Oh, precious, young Mary, God had His hand on you. Innocently you trusted Him and were given grace to handle the gossiping tongues of the church ladies. With your reputation at stake, you walked in faith and held your head high.

Develop the courage of Esther, the faith of Mary, and the wisdom of Naomi. Check your priorities, and remember Domestic-Diva Martha, Deceived Eve, and Salty Mrs. Lot.

If you learn from these biblical ladies and seek out modern-day WOW, your life will sparkle and shine. The greatest gift we can give to ourselves and to others is to set a bright example.

If you have tucked the lessons in this book into your heart, I have good news for you. Your future is so bright you will need sunglasses for all the sparkle and shine. As a humorist, there is no way I can conclude this book without sharing some of my favorite stories. I believe that adding a snort or two from some good old-fashioned church humor will help you keep your joy. You can't make this stuff up!

Mary's Flip-Flop: Personally speaking, I would have requested a better form of transportation to Bethlehem.

Mary's Sparkle and Shine: Being the mother of our Savior, she willingly embraced a life filled with tears, fears, and cheers.

How can you shine in the midst of your mess-ups? Take advice from Mary's shine—embrace a life filled with tears, fears, and cheers.

"A sense of humor . . . is needed armor. Joy in one's heart and some laughter on one's lips is a sign that the person down deep has a pretty good grasp of life."[57]

Hugh Sidey

Chapter 11

Laughter in the Pews

*Our mouths were filled with laughter,
our tongues with songs of joy. Then it
was said among the nations, "The
Lord has done great things for them."*
(Psalm 126:2 NIV)

CHANNEL 57

There was a sweet, godly couple who loved to serve the Lord. Their names were Joanne and Jimmy Thompson, and they were pioneers with television ministry. I know as I type this story they are enjoying their heavenly reward for their ministry and faithfulness.

Thomas and I were invited to share our faith and music many times on their show. During one particular appearance, Jimmy was interviewing us live on camera. Suddenly out of nowhere, Jimmy's voice lowered. He looked at me with great passion and asked, "Jane, have you and Thomas had miracles in your life?"

No, I thought to myself, but in the eighties everybody had some sort of miracle. Jimmy's eyes were fixated on me during the pregnant pause. I had to say something.

"Oh yes," I replied with a confident tone.

Then the unthinkable. "Tell us about it," Jimmy said.

I did not know what to say. Then it came to me. I turned, looked at Thomas, and said, "Tell him about it, Thomas."

Little did I know that at the same time I was professing miracles, Thomas was thinking, *What in the world is she going to say?*

I have no idea what came out of Thomas's mouth, but he did not call me out or get angry. It was our first miracle.

On another occasion, Jimmy's producer signaled me over from the couch to a little white fence where I stood to sing. I carefully removed my lavalier mic and tiptoed over to the other part of the studio. The producer whispered to me, "After the prayer requests are prayed over, then you sing."

I signaled my understanding with a thumbs-up, trying to be quiet and respect Jimmy, who was praying over the large stack of requests. I closed my eyes. Wearing five-inch heels, I thought to steady myself by holding on to the white picket fence. As soon as I reached to grab the fence, I realized it was not secured. Suddenly, the quiet of the moment was replaced by a huge crashing sound that made everyone jump. I opened one eye and watched hundreds of slips of paper floating in midair. I only wish I had sung "I'll Fly Away."

THE PROBLEM

There was a time when Thomas and I traveled across a few states sharing our faith. I call this our BC (before children) days. This coincided with Thomas changing professions from farming to financial services. With the main office located in Charlotte, North Carolina, Thomas had plenty of time to drive and listen to motivational tapes—specifically, Zig Ziglar. I actually knew Zig.

His words and unique twist on life always fascinated me. His analogies were particularly interesting to listen to but hard to repeat since only Zig knew how to get his point across. Thomas, however, should have stayed with listening to Zig since sharing "Ziglets" can be risky. We found this to be true when we spoke at a large, packed Baptist church in Easley, South Carolina.

I thought Thomas looked so handsome with his dark hair against the watermelon-colored (not pink) jacket he was wearing. He had an unusual twinkle in his eyes that Sunday evening. Suddenly, he leaned over and said, "I want to speak first. I heard a great message from Zig Ziglar and I want to share it. I feel led by the Spirit." Well, how can you argue with that? But, for some reason, his trancelike appearance concerned me.

"Friends," Thomas said with great compassion, "we have a crisis in America." A chorus of whispered Amens spread through the large sanctuary. I had heard the story, and I remembered how Zig set it up with the punch line of the size of our brains using the space between our ears as the analogy...in that order.

Then Thomas proceeded to have his Zig Ziglar moment in reverse. "We have a six-inch problem," Thomas continued.

Hmm, I thought. *That sounds a little weird.*

Then Thomas used his hands as some sort of measuring device and continued. "Let's be honest, some of us have more, and there are others who, unfortunately, have less."

Just for the record, I am not the sort of person whose mind is in the gutter, but from the look on the face of the minister, the body language of the deacons, and the gasps of the majority of the congregation, I was on their page.

Thomas continued: "I guess you are wondering what I am talking about." You could feel the suspense. Thankfully Thomas concluded with "it's the space between our ears."

With that line, I heard a series of comments: "Oh my," "Heavens above," and a loud good-ole-boy shout, "Praise the Lord!"

My clueless, godly husband sat down by me and said, "Did you hear the comments? I must have really touched their hearts."

"Go farther south," I commented, trying to control myself. After repeating his words back to him, I watched as Thomas's face, no kidding, turned the color of his jacket.

That was the last time Thomas used the brain-ear analogy, and come to think of it, it was the last time we were invited to that church.

I GOT THE DEVIL IN ME

Our minister, Steve, got a surprise one morning. There was a knock on the parsonage door, which is not un-common for preachers, but this one signaled the beginning of quite an adventure. "Preacher, I got the devil in me!" exclaimed the stranger to our minister.

So Steve prayed for the man.

"Thank you," replied the stranger. "Preacher, can you do me a favor?" he asked.

"Sure," answered Steve, putting his prayer into action.

"Can you drive me to a convenience store? I don't have a car," the stranger said.

So off they went. The man went into the store and when he got back into the car, he exclaimed once again, "Oh, Preacher, pray for me. I got the devil in me!"

So Steve prayed again.

"Preacher, can you help me some more?" the man asked. "I need a ride to another store." Well, Steve wanted to help this man, so off they went to another store and even another store. After several hours of taking this man to different convenience stores, Steve finally said, "Look, I am glad to help you, but I have to get back to the church."

The next morning there was a knock on the door. When Steve opened the door, he was surprised to see two police officers.

"Can I help you?" asked Steve.

"Yes," replied one officer. "We are looking for the driver of a car matching the description of your car that was involved in three robberies yesterday."

Later, Steve commented to me, "And to think I was trying to help that man get into the Pearly Gates and it almost sent me to the prison gates."

PEDALIN' TO HEAVEN

I was privileged to sing at Reverend Lowell Clark's memorial celebration. I have always loved his family and especially his wonderful wife, Miss Ada. She taught both of my children in preschool and is definitely a WOW.

The minister opened the service by saying, "Lowell preached his own funeral . . . by the way he lived his life." The quaint country church showcased Mr. Lowell's life in a visual tribute that included his iconic bicycle decorated with flowers, a worn Bible, and a Clemson University flag. Mr. Lowell loved to ride his bike and share his faith. What a way to cruise through life. Yes, we were celebrating the life of an amazing man.

With respect for Mr. Lowell's long life and the presence of many of his friends, the congregation was given the opportunity to speak about his life. Some who spoke made the congregation laugh out loud with comments like, "Lowell could put one on ya…and you couldn't get it off."

One story shared was a trick he played on Miss Ada. Mr. Lowell tied a clear fishing line around one of their daughter's dolls. With the life-sized doll placed at the top of the staircase, Mr. Lowell positioned himself on the last step. He called for Miss Ada to watch how well their toddler son had learned to walk down the stairs. Miss Ada turned her head and was practically hysterical when she saw her young son tumbling headfirst as Mr. Lowell yanked the undetected fishing line.

The next story was told by a bald-headed gentleman named, no kidding, Pee-Wee, who spoke of Mr. Lowell and his involvement as a Mason. At a large gathering of Masons, Mr. Lowell was asked to open the meeting in prayer. Before he began praying, he asked his buddy Pee-Wee to stand. Mr. Lowell announced to the entire crowd that he was sorry he and Pee-Wee were late coming to the event. Pee-Wee said he was surprised Lowell made that comment since they arrived in a timely manner. According to Pee-Wee, Mr. Lowell, always the prankster, continued.

"Y'all, please pray for my buddy Pee-Wee. He just had to roll down his window and his hairpiece blew off. We had to turn around and look for it. So if y'all see something lookin' like a dead possum on the interstate, it's probably Pee-Wee's hair."

As much as Pee-Wee tried to assure the crowd that he did not wear a hairpiece, Mr. Lowell was so convincing, many continued to comment throughout the day that they hoped he found his hair.

The funeral service concluded with the heartfelt words from a fellow minister Mr. Lowell had mentored: "I wonder what it's like to ride your bike on streets paved with gold."

So I ask, "Will your life preach your funeral?"

PRAYER REQUEST

I was attending my first Christian writers conference and chatting with some of my fellow attendees. We began sharing funny church stories that made all of us laugh out loud. Here is one of my favorite tales.

My fellow writer was a member of a Pentecostal Holiness Church that was having a Sunday night worship service dedicated to prayer. Attending the service was a lovely older woman who was visibly upset. Eager to share her prayer request, she waved her hand to be recognized by the minister.

"I am standing in the gap for my friend Mrs. Chandler," said the distraught lady. "She has so many health problems, I don't know where to begin. Her husband ran out on her with another woman and her daughter has a sick baby."

"Oh, Sister, I can see you are upset, but you are a blessing to Mrs. Chandler," said the minister. "Why don't you come to the altar, and we will all be in prayer with you?"

So they prayed and prayed. The enemy was rebuked and put on guard; it was a fiery moment. As the sweet lady took her seat, the minister commented, "Please let us know how Mrs. Chandler is doing."

"Yes, I will," commented the much-relieved lady. "I will know tomorrow morning at eleven a.m."

"My goodness," said the minister. "Does she have a doctor's appointment?"

"Oh no," answered the lady. "That's when the show comes on."

WEDDING WOES

Thomas and I used to sing duets together. Did you catch that past-tense word? *Used* to. I fired him. Simply put, you cannot sing a duet with someone who doesn't know the words to the song.

We were asked to sing for a lovely wedding in upstate South Carolina. We had been visiting Myrtle Beach, so the four-hour trip gave us ample time to practice. Over and over again, we rehearsed that song. I even wrote out the words for him, just in case.

The wedding director informed us that we would be seated at the front of the church. We were told to sing as soon as the processional had concluded. So basically we were to perform our duet as soon as the bride finished walking down the aisle. Thomas and I would be visible during the entire service with the exception of a small palm tree...thank the Lord.

I was prepared. I had my little cheat sheet in front of me that was actually designed to help Thomas remember the words. Later in the service, I was also supposed to sing "The Lord's Prayer."

The wedding ceremony began; the bride floated down the aisle. It was showtime for Thomas and me. Right before the first dah, duhto, dah, dah, dah, I reminded Thomas *not* to look at the couple eyeball to eyeball and sing to them. My voice teacher taught me that trick years ago to help prevent going blank on the words.

Thomas completely ignored my advice. Staring right into the faces of the bride and groom, he was supposed to sing, "As you try to follow Jesus, every step along the way, you'll be growing a little bit stronger every single day..."[58]

I watched as Thomas, halfway through the lyrics, went blank. He may have been sharing from his heart but his brain had another plan. When I saw his bewildered facial expression, I knew the words had left him. I began pointing and tapping on the paper like some out-of-control chicken pecking corn. Thomas's eyes danced all over that piece of paper, but he could not find his place.

Then the unthinkable happened. Thomas wrote new lyrics to the song, words that made no sense: "As you try to follow Jesus every step along the way...you'll be growing, lowing, sowing, showing, glowing all the way..." Basically, he rhymed every word.

After the initial shock wore off, we sat down and started to laugh—the kind of laughter you cannot control. Thank God for that palm tree since it somewhat concealed our out-of-control behavior. We straightened ourselves out, or so we thought, but the elderly minister made a faux pas.

"Repeat after me," he said. "Wiff dis wing, I thee wed." That did it. Once again we crouched behind that palm, but this time Thomas held his breath. I could see the perspiration running down his neck, soaking his collar. Then the next unthinkable thing happened—Thomas let out a loud snort that rang through that sweet little Baptist church.

I wanted to kill him.

The only redeemable act was my singing "The Lord's Prayer." And sing I did. With the force from my toenails to my vocal cords, I sang with the energy and passion of Beverly Sills.

After the service, a sweet lady approached me and said, "Honey, I love that song."

"Oh, thank you," I said, thinking she was surely referring to "The Lord's Prayer."

"I ain't never heard it before," she said.

I thought to myself, *Seriously, you have never heard "The Lord's Prayer"?*

"Oh, that's in the Bible," I said politely. "You know, when the Scripture says, 'These are the words Jesus said.'"

"Well," she continued, "I ain't never read where Jesus said 'growing, lowing, sowing, showing, glowing...'"

Thinking fast and walking away even faster, I said, "Oh, it's in that new translation."

Yes, that is the reason I fired Thomas.

EAGER EGGER

At one time, Thomas was part owner of a stockyard. I was recruited to work in the office adding bills. I hated it. Although I have a college degree and attended graduate school, I received a big, fat F in operating a calculator. Some of the women I sat with were the most brilliant women I have ever met. They could eat a sandwich, talk on the phone, and operate the calculator at the same time.

What I loved about these ladies were their stories, particularly the fearless and always entertaining mother-daughter duo of Faye and Lisa.

Let me set the scene. Imagine this entire conversation spoken with a calm tone and no emotion.

"Hey, Momma," said Lisa. "Did I tell you that Kinsli won the prize at the Baptist Church Easter egg hunt?"

"Uh-huh. That's good," said Faye, the proud grand-mother. "Did she find the golden egg?"

"No, she won because she had the most eggs. You know how competitive she is. She couldn't find any more eggs around the church so she went down the hill to that swamp. Kinsli got her some more eggs from a water moccasin's nest," continued Lisa.

"Yep, that's my girl," exclaimed Faye.

I about fell out of my chair.

I have no idea how that child turned out as an adult, but I bet she is successful in her chosen field. If she can collect snake eggs as a child, she can handle poisonous people.

SUPER-DUPER SENIORS

I was tired. After speaking for an association in beau-tiful sunny Florida, I arrived home only to head off for another speaking engagement. I had literally dropped my luggage at the house, picked up a few items, and left again. Frankly, I was angry at myself for accepting the engagement to speak and sing for a Valentine's banquet. I had just enjoyed a two-night stay in a fabulous re-sort in South Florida but was now on my way to speak in an all-purpose building located somewhere off Interstate 20.

I arrived in plenty of time to get set up and was greeted by several elderly men. They all wanted to help me with my equipment, but there was no way these men could lift a thing. It was borderline annoying since these Southern gents insisted on helping me.

I was also instructed to sit at the head table, which is not one of my favorite things to do since all eyes are on you. Ugh.

The nicely decorated building began filling up with many couples who interrupted my setting-up to express their appreciation for my presence at the banquet. I told myself, *Get a better attitude. These elderly folks have probably been planning this banquet for months, maybe even a year.*

The room was packed with smiling faces as the servers weaved around the long tables. Then a most unusual thing happened. The gentleman in charge stood up, tapped on his glass, and said, "The first order of business is to recognize all of the Hos. Would all of the Hos please stand?"

One by one, all the women in the room enthusiastically stood to their feet, smiling and waving like pageant queens. The elderly gentleman continued. "Where is the head Ho?" On the opposite side of the table, a lovely woman stood to her feet. Everyone cheered.

The wheels in my brain began to churn. I wondered, *Where am I and who are these people?*

The lady next to me leaned over and proudly proclaimed, "I was head Ho last year. You have no idea how difficult it is to keep all of these men happy."

In addition to my brain churning, my head began to spin. I was in the middle of a bunch of elderly people, trying to understand what was going on.

"Sooooo, y'all are the Hos?" I asked hesitantly. I had a feeling they had no idea what they were saying.

"Well, we call ourselves the *Hose* Circle. Actually, our officially name is the Panty Hose Circle."

That evening I fell in love with a crowd of wonderful Super Seniors. That speaking engagement in Florida paled in comparison to these appreciative folks who knew how to laugh, love, and celebrate life.

THE EASTER PAGEANT

Just because your church is small does not mean you cannot have a large worship experience. Our small church, Harmony UMC, decided to throw a last-minute Easter pageant. Faithful Harmonites wrote the script, made costumes, and decorated the church for reenacting the Passion of the Christ.

Our cast consisted of Wendell portraying Jesus; Joe Ben and Brad as the Roman soldiers; and a few congregants as the angry mob.

Sweet Genna, wife of one of the Roman soldiers, must have been inspired by the popular show *Saturday*

Night Live. Wearing bathrobes, Genna literally topped off their costumes with massive pointed tinfoil hats. Joe Ben and Brad looked like *SNL*'s Coneheads. To be honest, it was hard to take them seriously.

Wendell, portraying Jesus, forgot to buy some fake blood, so someone ran over to the fellowship hall and poured ketchup on him.

With the lights dimmed and the smell of McDonald's in the air, the Passion play began. Several in the angry mob were planted in the congregation. Those sitting around one "mobster" were not informed there would be an outburst of angry cries. Suddenly Betty, wife of the man portraying Jesus, stood to her feet, on cue, and yelled, "Crucify him!" In hindsight, the wife of the man portraying Jesus was not a good choice to yell "crucify him."

One congregant, not knowing this was part of the script, was so taken aback that she thought Wendell and Betty had had an argument. She exclaimed loudly, "What is wrong with you?"

To add to the drama, our minister was having some memory issues. He instructed the congregation to light their candles, but we had no candles. Being a faithful church member, I hurriedly made my way to the closet filled with our church supplies. I opened a dark closet and spotted a box of candles. Hesitantly, I reached into the dark closet. As I fished out the much-burned candles, I was amazed by how many small, black wicks were in that box. On closer inspection, I realized that those were not burned candlewicks—they were mouse droppings!

You know the saying *the show must go on*. As we were lighting the candle nubs with protective paper underneath, our minster made an unwise suggestion. "If you feel led of the Lord to speak, please do."

Now, our little church is old and historic. Burning candles is always a risk. But leave it to Thomas to be inspired to *share*. And share he did. He could not see me making gestures to hurry up; most of the candles had burned down to the little square paper. One shy friend of mine, who will remain nameless ('cause he would never speak to me again if I mentioned his name), ever so gently and discreetly tried to blow the candle out. Quietly blowing out his candle created a towering inferno like I have never seen. To say the least, we went off script.

The last image I have of that Easter Passion play was two Roman soldiers with pointed tinfoil hats, and Jesus drenched with Heinz ketchup stomping the floor to get the fire out.

All things considered, it was a success. We decided that the Holy Spirit made a surprise appearance in the final scene.

PUCKER UP

Some of the best humor comes from folks who are in the "people" business—more specifically, ministers.

Our little country church hit the preacher jackpot when Wayne and Esther Horne were assigned to a four-year appointment. We instantly fell in love with this young couple and their two adorable children.

Wayne came to see me in the hospital right after Caroline was born. In the middle of Wayne's beautiful prayer for my new arrival, I started to heave—and hurl. Before Wayne could say, "In Jesus' name," he grabbed the little pink plastic bowl and in one swoop, held it under my chin. With his other hand, he handed me a tissue. I don't think he missed a beat. It was like he had taken a course in seminary to handle such emergencies. Wayne and I bonded.

Wayne's wife, Esther, had a contagious laugh that seemed to make the sun shine on a stormy day. I loved her stories.

Esther told of one occasion when she and Wayne visited a young couple and their newborn baby. Wayne held the infant with tender care, enjoying every minute. Upon departure, the mother was caressing the child in a cradling position.

"Oh, how precious," exclaimed Wayne. "I just have to kiss her on the head one more time."

With his lips puckered up, he made his way down and made contact with what he thought was the baby's bald head. Suddenly he realized that he was not kissing the child's head. The mother was nursing. He confessed later that he thought the baby's "soft spot" was rather large.

On his way up, Esther said you could feel the heat radiating from Wayne's bloodred, embarrassed face. The father of the newborn, realizing Wayne's embarrassment, put his hand on Wayne's shoulder and said, "Well, Preacher, it could be worse. Coulda been twins."

BLING—BELIEVE, LOVE OTHERS, INVEST IN YOURSELF, NEVER GIVE UP, GIVE BACK

As I look back on my life, I have a passion for the *merry heart* that is mentioned in Proverbs 17:22. In the same manner, as I conclude my presentations, I like to send off my audiences with a smile.

Flip-flops happen. Just like the iconic biblical women I have written about, we all have events that turn our lives upside down and inside out. I believe the best way to handle these changes is to learn from wise women of yesterday and today. Adding in a good dose of humor will lift your spirits; it will give you a new vision concerning those issues because you will see them from a different perspective.

When you close this book, find or craft the most beautiful pair of rhinestone flip-flops possible. And every time you have a tough trial, find those shoes. But here is my challenge to you: don't wear them right away. I believe you must first handle the flip-flops to be able to wear the flip-flops. The most important lesson you can teach yourself and others is how to sparkle and shine as you go through mess-ups and challenges.

Let those shoes be a physical reminder of the lessons highlighted in the lives of our biblical mentors.

Grab some superglue and a handful of sequins, rhinestones, rubies, and pearls. Create a blinding sparkle. Bling up your life from the tip of your toes to the top of your head with forgiveness, courage, godly balance, and wisdom. Always remember...when life flips, don't be a flop!

Acknowledgments

A special thank-you to my agent, Les Stobbe, for his guidance in crafting my vision for this book and helping me handle the flip-flops of rejection from many publishers. God bless FaithWords, a division of the Hachette Book Group, and senior editor Keren Baltzer for seeing the vision of Christian humor relating to the mess-ups of both biblical and modern-day women in our search to discover extravagant joy. I am thankful for the fabulous FaithWords team for allowing me to bug them practically every day. A big shout-out to my editor friend Denise Loock for her vision and to Nicci Jordan Hubert for her superb edits in keeping "my voice" and challenging me to dig deeper.

To my husband, Thomas, who allows me to do crazy things as I write books and travel the country as an inspirational humorist speaker.

I would like to thank all of my fabulous flip-flop friends who helped me when I tripped, stumbled, and was brought to my knees. They picked me up, prayed for me, and helped me find my shine with renewed faith and determination to add rhinestones to my flip-flops. What a blessing to share my shine with my audiences through my books and presentations with love, joy, and laughter.

Maybe my fabulous flip-flop friends and I can finally plan a beach trip, wear our flip-flops, cry, pray, drink coffee, share a glass of wine/whine and, when not shopping, stay in our pj's most of the day.

Notes

1. http://fablesofaesop.com/the-farmer-and-the-snake.html.

2. Robert Driskell, *What Christians Want to Know.* Copyright© 2010–2015. Telling Ministries LLC, www.whatchristianswantto know.com/what-was-life-like-in-the-garden-of-eden-before-sin/.

3. Yip Harburg, "The Begat," *Finian's Rainbow* (1947).

4. Lisa Cummings, CEO of Pinch Yourself Careers, quoted in Ian Altman's "Don't Waste Time Fixing Your Weaknesses," *Forbes* Magazine.

5. http://christianchat.com/miscellaneous/134185biscuits.html; http://www.uglyhedgehog.com/t-365579-1.html.

6. http://scotthansenconsulting.com/only-10-people-will-cry-at-your-funeral/.

7. All-Creatures.org. Copyright 1998–2015. The Mary T. and Frank L. Hoffman Family Foundation. www.all-creatures.org/hr/what-12.htm.

8. *My Big Fat Greek Wedding*. Directed by Joel Zwick. Gold Circle Films. 2002.

9. Elizabeth Fletcher, *Women in the Bible*. Copyright 2006.

10. www.crosswalk.com/faith/women/6-powerful-life-lessons-from-the-book-of-esther.html.

11. www.whatchristianswanttoknow.com/sarah-in-the-bible-character-profile-and-life-story/.

12. Ibid.

13. www.biblegateway.com/resources/all-men-bible/Isaac.

14. www.behindthename.com/name/ishmael.

15. www.biblegateway.com/resources/all-women-bible/Lot-8217-s-Wife.

16. www.lizcurtishiggs.com/bad-girls-of-the-bible-lots-wife /#sthash.88KvKZfa.dpuf.

17. "Ding-Dong! The Witch Is Dead" (https://en.wikipedia.org/wiki /Ding-Dong!_The_Witch_Is_Dead) is the centerpiece of several individual songs in an extended set-piece performed by the Munchkin characters Glinda (Billie Burke) and Dorothy Gale (Judy Garland) in the classic 1939 film *The Wizard of Oz*. It was composed by Harold Arlen, with the lyrics written

by E. Y. Harburg. *The Wizard of Oz* is a 1939 American musical comedy-drama fantasy film produced by Metro-Goldwyn-Mayer and the most well-known and commercially successful adaptation based on the 1900 novel *The Wonderful Wizard of Oz* by L. Frank Baum.

18. This song is also known as "If I Only Had a Heart" and "If I Only Had the Nerve," Harold Arlen (music) and E. Y. Harburg (lyrics). https://en.wikipedia.org/wiki/If_I_Only_Had_a_Brain 1939 film *The Wizard of Oz*.

19. www.fcfi.org/home/about-fcfi.

20. www.fcfi.org/home/about-fcfi/walking-stick-story/.

21. Charles R. Swindoll, *The Grace Awakening* (Nashville: Thomas Nelson, 2006).

22. www.sharefaith.com/guide/christian-ministries /Women%20in%20the%20Bible/Naomi-Guides-Ruth-to-Boaz.html.

23. Bob Deits, *Life After Loss: A Practical Guide to Renewing Your Life After Experiencing Major Loss,* 5th ed. (Da Capo Lifelong Books, 2009), 117–118.

24. www.sharefaith.com/guide/christian-ministries/Women% 20in%20the%20Bible/Naomi-Guides-Ruth-to-Boaz.html.

25. www.jw.org/en/publications/books/true-faith/ruth-and-naomi /#link0.

26. www.biblestudytools.com/bible-stories/ruth-and-naomi
    .html.

27. www.shmoop.com/ruth/debates.html-ruth.

28. Oxford Bible, p. 192.

29. www.shmoop.com/ruth/debates.html-ruth.

30. https://en.wikipedia.org/wiki/The_Church_Lady.

31. http://hawaiitribune-herald.com/news/features/why-did-gandhi-
    say-if-it-weren-t-christians-i-d-be-christian.

32. www.lords-prayer-words.com/famous_prayers
    /god_grant_me_the_serenity.html.

33. http://alltimeshortstories.com/inspirational-the-black-dot.

34. www.poetrynation.com/poem.php?id=50509.

35. www.jamesaltucher.com/2013/12/the-5x5-trick-to-make-life-
    better/.

36. https://www.womanon.com/story/whats-your-favorite-nickname-
    for-a-hot-flash.

37. Quotes from Marshall's book *Healthy Living*.

38. Sent to author in email from Margaret Marshall, August 25,
    2016.

39. To the tune of "If You're Happy and You Know it, Clap Your
    Hands!" Isaak Dunayevsky, "Molodejnaya," 1938 Soviet film
    Volga-Volga.

40. http://www.salary.com/2016-mothers-day-infographics/.

41. "Yesterday." Songwriters John Lennon and Paul McCartney. Published by Lyrics © Sony/ATV Music Publishing LLC.

42. Adult Bible Studies, Winter 2016–17 "Creation: A Divine Cycle," p.15 Adam Hamilton, Cokesbury, goo.gl/YAV3i0.

43. Immaculée Ilibagiza, *Left to Tell: Discovering God Amidst the Rwandan Holocaust* (Carlsbad, CA: Hay House, 2014), 101. Available at www.amazon.com/Left-Tell-Discovering-Rwandan-Holocaust /dp/1401944329/.

44. Penny Hunt, *Bounce, Don't Break: Stories, Reflections, and Words of Encouragement Through Times of Change* (Raleigh, NC: Straight Street Books, 2015), 103. Available at www.amazon.com/Bounce-Dont-Break-reflections-encouragement/dp/1941103707/.

45. www.bible.com/uk/bible/585/mat.25.gulnt.

46. https://baptiststoday.org/a-remarkable-woman/.

47. www.biblegateway.com/resources/all-women-bible/Anna.

48. http://justus.anglican.org/resources/bcp/1928/HC.htm.

49. www.amazon.com/Nordies-Noon-Personal-Stories-Breast-ebook /dp/0738211125.

50. www.msn.com/en-us/lifestyle/smart-living/45-life-lessons-written-by-a-90-year-old-woman/ar-BBhwKAN.

51. www.entrepreneur.com/article/225131.

52. https://twitter.com/thezigziglar/status/684026500891316225.

53. www.imdb.com/character/ch0000184/quotes.

54. www.christianitytoday.com/women/2009/december/real-problem-
    with-marys-baby-bump.html.

55. Ibid.

56. Ibid.

57. www.goodreads.com/author/quotes/107737.Hugh_Sidey.

58. "Only the Beginning" by Bob & Joy Cull from Windborne.
    www.youtube.com/watch?v=CWh-eEbStuY.

About the Author

With a sense of humor and hard work, Jane Jenkins Herlong traveled from her family farm to the runway of the Miss America Pageant all the way to performing at Radio City Music Hall. Combining humor, truth, and her award-winning singing, Jane crisscrosses the country teaching her audiences how to work smart, laugh often, and live their dreams. She is also a Sirius XM humorist and award-winning author and professional singer, as well as a recent inductee into the prestigious CPAE Speaker Hall of Fame. Find out more at janeherlong.com.